7

NORTH ADAMS

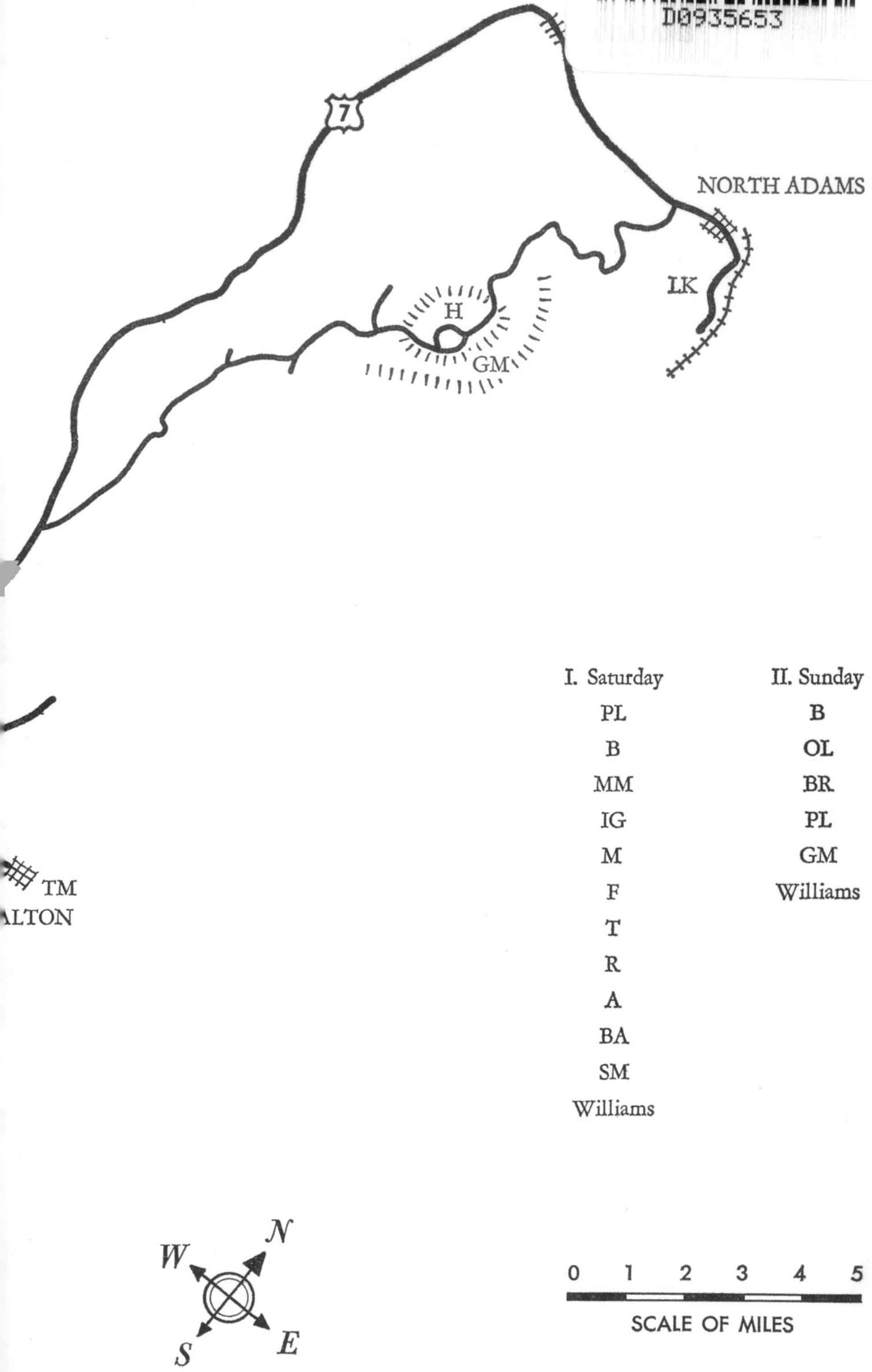

LK

H

GM

TM

ALTON

I. Saturday	II. Sunday
PL	B
B	OL
MM	BR
IG	PL
M	GM
F	Williams
T	
R	
A	
BA	
SM	
Williams	

0 1 2 3 4 5

SCALE OF MILES

MELVILLE AND HAWTHORNE IN THE BERKSHIRES

Edited by Howard P. Vincent

Henry A. Murray Luther Stearns Mansfield
Jeanne C. Howe Morse Peckham John D. Seelye
Maurita Willett J. Donald Crowley John H. McElroy
Albert McLean F. DeWolfe Miller Edwin S. Shneidman

MELVILLE
&
HAWTHORNE
IN THE BERKSHIRES

A SYMPOSIUM
Melville Annual 1966

The Kent State University Press

KENT STUDIES IN ENGLISH
General Editor, Howard P. Vincent

I. *Essays on Determinism in American Literature*
Edited by Sydney J. Krause

II. *The Computer and Literary Style*
Edited by Jacob Leed

III. *Bartleby, The Scrivener: The Melville Annual*
Edited by Howard P. Vincent

IV. *Mark Twain and the Backwoods Angel*
By William Spengemann

V. *Reality's Dark Dream: Dejection in Coleridge*
By Beverly Fields

VI. *Wordsworth: The Construction of a Personality*
By Wallace W. Douglas

VII. *Melville and Hawthorne in the Berkshires*
Edited by Howard P. Vincent

Library of Congress Card Catalog Number 68-18936

Manufactured in the United States of America
at the press of The Oberlin Printing Company
Designed by Merald E. Wrolstad
First Edition

A Prefatory Note

THIS VOLUME incorporates most of the talks delivered at the Melville-Hawthorne Conference held at Williamstown and Pittsfield, Massachusetts over the Labor Day weekend of 1966. Although for various reasons three of those talks have not been included, two papers written since that time have been added for the sake of filling in the regional and topographical details necessary in understanding the environment in which the two authors met and moved.

The paper by Maurita Willett was awarded first prize in a special essay contest whose high quality called for many prizes not actually given.

When the Kent Studies in English issued the first Melville Annual, *Bartleby the Scrivener: A Symposium*, I expressed the concern that that book might have been "setting a standard difficult to maintain." That fear has been allayed.

H. P. V.

Contents

HENRY A. MURRAY

1. Prelude

IN THE FLAGWAVING part of his extravaganza in praise of the as-yet-unappreciated "rich and rare stuff" in Hawthorne, Melville exhorted his fellow-countrymen to cherish and glorify their authors. And now, as if in compliance with his urgings, here we are, a century or so later, drawn together mostly because we cherish, each in his own way, the rich and rare stuff in the works of both of these American greats, the praiser and the praised. It remains to be seen whether at the end of our 3-day gam, it will be announced by the angelic voices that we have done more to reduce or to enhance their glory, to obscure or to clarify their intentions, to accent the worse or the better shows of their symbolic craftmanship.

Their names have been coupled in the title of this conference, first, because in certain important respects their writings may be coupled, for instance, by their shared preoccupation with what Melville called "the tragicalness of human thought in its own unbiased, native, and profounder workings;" and second, because during the year and a quarter at the turn of the mid-century in which they both resided in the Berkshires, each at the peak of his creative power, they were coupled in friendship on a deep level of asymmetrical communication, uttered and unuttered. As you all know, when they first met in Stockbridge at the home of David Dudley Field, Hawthorne was forty-six years of age, Melville thirty-one. The elder author, after publishing three volumes in 25 years, had just recently delivered himself of his acknowledged masterpiece; the younger one was in the throes of his, after publishing six volumes in 5 years. *The Scarlet Letter* had won immediate and unanimous approbation. *Moby-Dick*, on the other hand, would be fearlessly and fatefully shaped, during the ensuing year, for contemporary disapprobation; and throughout that span of stupendous creative exuberance the "divine magnet" was on the as-yet-unrivaled Hawthorne, and the magnet of his young admirer and challenger responded.

Our program for this week-end is more diversified than is customary for meetings of this kind. Besides enlightening intakes by way of our ears emanating from some of the foremost discerners of the unique characteristics and accomplishments of one or the other of these two magnets, we are being offered numerous intakes by way of our eyes emanating from certain localities associated, at one time or another, with their activities as well as from several elegantly arranged exhibits of their works and other pertinent memorabilia, and then, as a special treat, delightful intakes by way of both eyes and ears of a musical and dramatic nature, not to speak of intakes by way of a larger channel which should be nourishing on the chemical level and possibly intoxicating.

For the planning of this schedule of multifarious enjoyments, involving, as it did, countless respectable toils, trials, and tribulations, we are indebted, from first to last, to our exceedingly zealous, devoted, and indefatigable secretary, Howard Vincent, as well as to the Berkshire members of our incomparable committee, each and every one of them, but chiefly, of course, to its chairman, Luther Mansfield, on whose broad shoulders ultimately reposed the burden of responsibility for the entire complex enterprise. My own contribution was merely to suggest some time ago—never mind how long precisely—that the grand program of Providence for the predestinated conclave should allow sufficient time to rove about a little and see the green, golden, and historic parts of the surrounding Berkshire world; and although the role of dragoman for this outdoor, foot-loose, non-intellectual portion of the week-end was originally assigned to me, in the end it was Luther Mansfield who performed most of the necessary duties. And so it is meet and right that I should transfer to him, with your permission, all the honor and the glory of the office of President.

There is a certain irony in the fact that the coupling of the eventually estranged Hawthorne and Melville, the two most in-going and seclusive of American authors, should have pulled together here from various parts of the world, by gravitational affinity, what may be the largest number of men and women ever to be assembled in this country in the name of one or two authors. With what medley of ambiguous emotions would you suppose—self-consciousness, embarrassment, pride, joyous exultation, modesty, skepticism, antipathy, or indifference—is the ghost of each of these fame-enamoured men viewing us at this moment? Hawthorne, I am sure, shyly from the church steeple, and Melville, maybe, in our midst, taking our pulses to see if we are true.

Since I happen to be one of those eccentric Americans who thinks that three people is a crowd, I was appalled when I heard of this expected multitude. My first thought was that Luther Mansfield wanted to show that the hospitality of Williams College was absolutely limitless. And then—there being no question about the prodigality of this exemplary institution—I began to suspect that he had designed an experiment with human beings, comparable to those recently performed with Norway rats, to demonstrate the disastrous, biological and behavioral effects of over-crowding. But he has assured me that he had no such intent and that the probability of deadly quarrels among the ladies and of miscarriages among the gentlemen is negligible. And so, as the titular but largely inoperative President of the Melville Society, I welcome every blessed one of you with some confidence that, in one way or another, this 3-day reunion will prove fruitful to you all.

LUTHER STEARNS MANSFIELD

2. *Melville and Hawthorne in the Berkshires*

EPISTLE DEDICATORY—to Summer Ramblers on the Berkshire Hills. Friends:

From Vermont upon the north to Connecticut upon the south, for fifty miles along the eastern borders of New York, extends Berkshire, the most western county of Massachusetts. It is a region of hills and valleys, of lake and stream, of woodland, farm and field. Its beauty is world renowned; for the pens of Bryant and Miss Sedgwick have made it their favorite theme. Within its limits are Monument Mountain, Icy Glen, the Stockbridge Bowl, Green River, with a thousand other scenes of storied or of unsung loveliness.

In the north rise majestically, three thousand five hundred feet into the air, the double peaks of Greylock. Along our western borders lie the dome-like summits of the Taghconic range. Less graceful in outline, but even more romantic with broken and precipitous ascents, the Hoosacs shut out the world upon the east. Within this moutain walled amphitheatre lies the upland valley of the Housatonic, with all its fertile farms, its mansion homes, and frequent villages. . . . If the traveler. . . . asks for a retreat among wild and picturesque scenery, adorned by much that is pleasant and refined in his city life, but far removed from its heat and turmoil; where he can draw closer the silken cord of social intercourse, and yet throw loose some of its galling chains; where nature ennobles by her greatness but never chills with a frown, he may find it all amid the varied beauty of the Berkshire Hills.

Thus J. E. A. Smith, the young poet friend of the Melvilles and the Morewoods, writing under the pseudonym of "Godfrey Greylock," prefaced his volume, *Taghconic* (1852). For the revised 1879 edition of this book, to the third sentence above naming Bryant and Catherine Maria Sedgwick, he added:

> . . . and in later years Holmes and Longfellow, Hawthorne, Melville and Thoreau have invested it with the halo of their genius.

And now in September 1966 some two hundred Melville and Hawthorne scholars, like wise men following the halo these authors have hung in the sky, have gathered to visit some of these Berkshire glories and to do special honor to two of the literary ramblers through these hills a century ago. It is appropriate that you should tarry first in the northern end of the county, which Hawthorne visited in 1838 at much this same season of the year.

Arriving 26 July, Hawthorne spent some weeks in North Adams in 1838. He climbed Greylock several times; he inspected lime-kilns on the slopes; he noted in his journal the amused reactions of a tavern crowd to an old German with a diorama, whose "gigantic, brown, hairy hand," seen through the glass as he guided attention to details of his pictures, seemed "the Hand of Destiny"; he recorded also the antics of a dog furiously chasing his tail, "as if one half of his body were at deadly enmity with the other"—all details later worked into "Ethan Brand."

Hawthorne also attended the Williams College commencement exercises on 15 August, and made some observations strangely snobbish for a graduate of rural Bowdoin:

> At the tavern, students, with ribbons, pink or blue, fluttering from their buttonholes—these being the badges of rival societies. A considerable gathering of people, chiefly arriving in wagons or buggies—some barouches—very few chaises. The most characteristic part of the scene was where the pedlers, gingerbread-sellers &c were collected, a few hundred yards from the meeting-house. . . . A good many people were the better or worse for liquor. . . . The people here show out their character much more strongly than they do with us:—there was not the quiet, silent, dull decency as in our public assemblages

> —but mirth, anger, eccentricity, all showing themselves freely. Many watermelons for sale, and people burying their muzzles deep in the juicy flesh of them. Cider. Beer. Many of the people had their mouths half opened in a grin, which more than anything else, I think, indicates a low stage of refinement . . . . Well dressed ladies in the meeting-house, in silks and cambrics—their sunburnt necks, in contiguity with the delicate fabric of the dress, showing the yeoman's daughter.

Since you are here at Williams, you will probably be most interested in what Hawthorne had to say about the students:

> Country graduates—rough, brown-featured, schoolmaster looking, half-bumpkin, half-scholar figures, in black ill-cut broadcloth;—their manners spoilt by what little of the gentleman there was in them. . . . They were a rough hewn, heavy set of fellows, from the hills and woods in this neighborhood; great unpolished bumpkins, who had grown up farmer-boys, and had little of the literary man, save green spectacles and black broadcloth—which all of them had not. Talking with a broad accent, and laughing bumpkinlike—and sheepishness overspreading all; together with a vanity at being students.

When some of the Williams students appeared the following day at the dinner table of the North Adams tavern where he lodged, Hawthorne was more favorably impressed by their "brotherly feeling for each other" and "half boyish, half manly character."

Williams College had come into being when the free school established in Williamstown in 1791 by the bequest of Col. Ephraim Williams (who had been killed at the battle of Lake George 1755) was granted a charter as an institution of collegiate rank in 1793. William Cullen Bryant, already the author of *The Embargo,* was briefly at Williams during 1810-1811, and the local tradition is that the unhappy student began *Thanatopsis* in nearby Flora's Glen. Few students came from very far away in the early days; Berkshire county furnished most of them. Mark Hopkins of Stockbridge, a graduate of 1824, soon returned to his alma mater as tutor, became a professor in 1830, and president from 1836 to 1872. It was not until his administration that Williams began to develop the reputation that made possible the achievement of the hope of the founders that "young men from every part of the Union" might resort there for instruction "in all the branches of useful and polite literature."

Mark Hopkins pioneered in making the student the center of the educational experience, and he did it so well that one of his former students, James A. Garfield, speaking to an alumni dinner in New York in 1871, immortalized his achievement in an aphorism that has passed into the lore of American education: "The ideal college is Mark Hopkins on one end of a log and a student on the other."

After a visit to Williams College in 1839, Thoreau was more charitable than Hawthorne, and remarked: "It would be no small advantage if every college were thus located at the base of a mountain." For Thoreau the location was "as good at least as one well-endowed professorship."

Hawthorne, however, was not unmindful of the scenic and scientific significance of Williams. Of his approach to the college town on the stage from Pittsfield in 1838, he recorded:

> I pointed to a hill some distance before us, and asked what it was. "That, Sir," said [the driver], "is a very high hill. It is known by the name of Graylock." He seemed to feel that this was a more poetical epithet than Saddleback, which is a more usual name for it. Graylock, or Saddleback, is quite a respectable moutain; and I suppose the former name has been given it, because it often has a gray cloud, or lock of gray mist upon his head; it does not ascend into a peak, but heaves up a round ball, and has supporting ridges on each side. Its summit is not bare, like Mt Washington, but covered with forest. The driver said, that several years since the students of Williams college erected a building for an observatory on the top of this mountain, and employed him to haul the materials for constructing it; and he was the only man that had ever driven an ox-team up Graylock. It was necessary to drive the team round and round, in ascending. President Griffin rode up on horseback.

It was in the ruins of this student-constructed building that Herman Melville and others of his family, the Duyckinck brothers, Mrs. Morewood and others spent the night of 11 August 1851, after a strenuous mountain climb and a floor-spread feast of ham and chicken, generously lubricated with Jamaica rum, port, cognac, and champagne. On that occasion, Evert A. Duyckinck described the structure:

> The Observatory. This is a structure some seventy feet high without which you would see nothing of the view, a jungle of trees skirting the ball. It was put up some twenty years since by the neighboring Williams College for observation on the winds &c but the Yankees broke the instruments and have well nigh plucked the building of its boards and stairways so that it's now a wind and rain penetrated and in important parts, a trembling affair. Ascending its crazy boards you see a near picture of sublime mountain desolation, and your distant acquaintances of Berkshire, the "Dome" of the Taconic, Monument Mt, Pontoosac Lake, &c &c with Vermont at your back, New York and the Catskills on the right, the Green Mountain chain on the left blue and thinly veiled in the afternoon heat.

These two passages linking the Williams building atop Mount Greylock with Hawthorne and Melville are almost the only surviving contemporary references to it. The college history says little about this meteorological observatory, but it was doubtless inspired by Professor Albert Hopkins, brother of the president, who—again aided by his students—in 1836-1838 built on the Williams campus the second (and the oldest surviving) astronomical observatory in the United States.

Herman Melville was probably never in Williamstown until after he became a resident of Pittsfield in 1850. But in various references to young collegians—especially in *Moby-Dick* and in *Pierre*—he almost certainly had in mind the students of Williams College.

Probably Hawthorne did not know that among the Williams Commencement crowd he laughed at in 1838 were several representatives of the later famous Field family of Stockbridge, assembled for the graduation of the youngest son, Henry Martyn Field, who was to become a celebrated minister and religious editor. The father, David Dudley Field, Sr., had been Mark Hopkins's pastor in his youth and college days, and had been awarded an honorary D.D. the year before by the young president. The eldest son, David Dudley Field, Jr., Williams class of 1825, had been from pre-college days one of the president's closest friends and for the next fifty years, as a leading alumnus, would work closely with him in building the modern Williams. Two other brothers were also graduates of Williams: Jonathan Edwards Field, salutatorian in 1832, and Stephen Johnson Field, valedictorian in 1837, who—after Lincoln's appointment of him in 1863—was to serve longer than any other man on the U.S. Supreme Court. Brother Cyrus West Field had bypassed college to begin early a money-making career that later would make possible his persistent but financially disastrous efforts to lay the Atlantic cable. For brother Timothy Beal Field, the sailor, a merchant ship was his Williams, as a whaleship was to serve Melville as his Yale College and his Harvard.

In 1838, when Hawthorne attended the Williams Commencement, David Dudley Field, Jr., was already a distinguished New York lawyer, and was soon to be the leading figure in revising both the civil and criminal codes of New York so that they would serve as a model for legal reform in other states and even for enactments by the British parliament. His son, David Dudley Field, the 3rd, was graduated from Williams 21 August 1850, and delivered the Philosophical Oration on "The Planet Neptune"; at the same exercises the father delivered the Alumni Oration and the grandfather pronounced the benediction.

For American literary history, however, David Dudley Field, Jr.'s most important function came sixteen days earlier than his son's graduation. It was his serving as host 5 August 1850 at the gathering of literary lions in his Stockbridge summer home, Laurel Cottage, for a three-hour turkey and roast beef dinner, "well moistened by the way." This was the occasion of the first meeting of Herman Melville and Nathaniel Hawthorne. Without Field there might be no occasion for such a conference as we are having here. It is fitting that what an alumnus of Williams College started, his alma mater should carry on.

Several people had a part in the making of this monumental feast, though Field was the chief administrator and the harmonizer of plans. The story is best told by a calendar of events.

Thursday, 1 August—John L. O'Sullivan, one-time editor of the *Democratic Review*, long-time friend of the Hawthornes, godfather of Una, and currently guest at the Red House in Lenox, drove the Hawthornes to Stockbridge to call on Mrs. Field. (O'Sullivan had worked with Field as a zealous partisan in the advocacy of legal reform.) It happened to be the night of a torchlight procession through the Ice Glen, and Mrs. Field invited them all to stay over for the affair. Mrs. Hawthorne and Una remained overnight, but the men and Julian returned to the Red House.

Friday, 2 August—On the evening train coming up from New York to Pittsfield to visit Melville, Evert A. Duyckinck and Cornelius Mathews met their fellow New Yorker, David Dudley Field, Jr., who issued the invitation for Monday, including Melville. Field apparently did not know Hawthorne, for he was not then mentioned as a possible guest. It was probably Duyckinck's thought that they might also drive up to Lenox for a visit to the Red House, for he knew Hawthorne well, and had served as his publisher.

Saturday, 3 August—Field and his wife drove to Lenox to call on the Hawthornes and to invite them both for dinner on Monday. Almost certainly this was the first time the two men had met. (The Hawthornes kept no horse or conveyance, and were dependent upon friends for transportation.)

Sunday, 4 August—The Hawthornes were the guests of James T. Fields (publisher of *The Scarlet Letter*) and his wife for dinner at the hotel in Lenox and afterward drove with them to Pittsfield to call on Oliver Wendell Holmes. Possibly they thus conveyed the Stockbridge invitation to him.

Monday, 5 August—Melville, Duyckinck, Mathews, and Holmes made the trip from Pittsfield to Stockbridge by the early morning train. Met at the station by their host, they went immediately to Laurel Cottage to meet his wife, his collegian son, and his seventeen-year-old daughter, Jeanie Lucinda Field. They had time for a brisk walk up Laurel Hill (or Sacrifice Mount, as it was sometimes called), almost in the backyard of their host, before Hawthorne, James T. Fields, and Mrs. Fields, who had driven the shorter distance from Lenox, arrived. (Mrs. Hawthorne did not attend.) Henry Dwight Sedgwick, Jr., a young New York lawyer but summer resident in Stockbridge, joined the party for the climb up Monument Mountain and for dinner. Joel Tyler Headley, the New York military historian, then staying at the local hotel, came in after dinner to lead the group through the Ice Glen.

In his account of the events of the day for the 31 August 1850 issue of the *Literary World*, Cornelius Mathews made it clear that there were twelve seated at the dinner table. Apparently young Field, the collegian, did not eat with the group. There was present, however, "a most lady-like and agreeable conversationist, mother of a distinguished democratic reviewer," seated at the hostess's right, who cannot be certainly identified; she may well have been the host's mother, since Field was an occasional contributor to the *Democratic Review*. (Obviously Mathews meant to identify her as mother of someone connected with that periodical.) Starting with Mrs. Field at one end of the table and continuing to her right, then, came first the unidentified "mother", next Hawthorne, Mrs. Fields, James T. Fields, Sedgwick; then the host at the far end, and on his right in order Evert A. Duyckinck, Jeanie Lucinda Field, Melville, Mathews, and Holmes. It is barely possible that the older lady was Sedgwick's widowed mother, Jane Minot Sedgwick, and that she is one and the same with the "tall Mrs. Sedgwick" with whom Duyckinck later in the day discussed *Hope Leslie*, the novel by her sister-in-law, Catherine Maria Sedgwick, in which the Pequod Indian maiden Magawisca makes the daring rescue of the young white boy, almost Pocahontas fashion, from the sacrifice rock on Laurel Hill, which some of the party had seen that morning.

James T. Fields, writing to Longfellow a few days after the Stockbridge party, merely listed the more important guests. In *Yesterdays with Authors*, published twenty-one years later, he was somewhat confused about the order of events, but gave fuller details:

> We scrambled to the top [of Monument Mountain] with great spirit, and when we arrived, Melville, I remember, bestrode a peaked rock, which ran out like a bowsprit, and pulled and hauled imaginary ropes for our delectation. Then we all assembled in a shady spot, and one of the party read to us Bryant's beautiful poem commemorating Monument Mountain. Then we lunched among the rocks, and somebody proposed Bryant's health, and "long life to the dear old poet." This was the most popular toast of the day, and it took, I remember, a considerable quantity of Heidseick to do it justice. In the afternoon, pioneered by Headley, we made our way, with

> merry shouts and laughter, through the Ice-Glen. Hawthorne was among the most enterprising of the merry-makers; and being in the dark much of the time, he ventured to call out lustily and pretend that certain destruction was inevitable to all of us. After this extemporaneous jollity, we dined . . . and Hawthorne rayed out in a sparkling and unwonted manner. I remember the conversation at table chiefly ran on the physical differences between present American and English men, Hawthorne stoutly taking part in favor of the American. This 5th of August was a happy day throughout, and I never saw Hawthorne in better spirits.

Probably Evert Duyckinck's letter to his wife, written the morning after the party, gave the most reliable account of what was done and said:

> . . . . we fell in line in three conveyances for Monument Mountain. You will find the legend and the poem in Bryant's poems. It is a rough projection of the cliffs, scarred and blasted. We took to our feet on its sides and strode upward Hawthorne and myself in advance, talking of the Scarlet Letter. As we scrambled over rocks at the summit which surveys a wide range of country on either side, a black thunder cloud from the south dragged its ragged edges toward us—the thunder rolling in the distance. They talked of shelter and shelter there proved to be though it looked unpromising but these difficulties, like others, vanish on trial and a few feet of rock with a damp underground of mosses and decay actually sheltered publisher Fields curled whiskers, his patent leathers and his brides delicate blue silk. Dr Holmes cut three branches for an umbrella and uncorked the champagne which was drunk from a silver mug. The rain did not do its worst and we scattered over the cliffs, Herman Melville to seat himself, the boldest of all, astride a projecting bowsprit of rock while Dr Holmes peeped about the cliffs and protested it affected him like ipecac. Hawthorne looked wildly about for the great carbuncle. Mathews read Bryant's poem. The exercise was glorious. We shed rain like ducks. . . . Then came the dinner—a three hour's business from turkey to ice cream, well moistened by the way. Dr Holmes said some of his best things and drew the whole company out by laying down various propositions

> of the superiority of the Englishman. Melville attacked him vigorously. Hawthorne looked on and Fields his publisher smiled with internal satisfaction underneath his curled whiskers at the good tokens of a brilliant poem from Holmes in a few days at the Yale College celebration [*Astrea*, delivered before the Phi Beta Kappa Society, 14 August 1850]. . . . It was a merciless thing to get us off from such a dinner in the afternoon to the Ice Glen, a break in one of the hills of tumbled huge, damp, mossy rocks in whose recesses ice is said to be found all the year round. Headley led the way. . . . Talk and tea and a tall Mrs. Sedgwick and a cross examination which I did not stand very well on Hope Leslie and Magawisca—and at 10 o'clock the railway home. . . .

Cornelius Mathews facetiously accused Holmes of maintaining that "in less than twenty years it would be a common thing to grow in these United States men sixteen and seventeen feet high; and intellectual in proportion." It would seem that the humor rather than the argument lingered longer with Fields. Clearly Duyckinck is right that it was Melville, not the shy Hawthorne, who was the chief challenger of Holmes, and his suggestion that the argument was serious at the core is borne out both by Holmes's poem and by Melville's next published writing.

Melville left no explicit account of the Stockbridge party, but "Hawthorne and his Mosses," appearing anonymously in the *Literary World*, 17 and 24 August 1850, reflected his response to the man of whom Duyckinck said, "Hawthorne is a fine ghost in a case of iron—a man of genius and he looks it and lives it." When Duyckinck returned to New York one week after the party, he took with him the manuscript of Melville's essay. It is unlikely that Melville's reading of the book and his writing were both done in a few scattered moments snatched from almost constant excursions and parties with his house guests of that busy week, but it is even more unlikely that a previously planned and partially or wholly written essay would not be significantly revised after the personal encounter with Hawthorne.

Of this momentous meeting Hawthorne's journal entry told only the names of those present, with bare mention of the before-dinner climb of Monument Mountain, the interruption by a shower, and the after-dinner scramble through the Ice Glen. But within a day or two he wrote to Horatio Bridge: "I met Melville, the other day, and like him so much that I have asked him to spend a few days with me before leaving these parts." Only three days after the Stockbridge party Melville called at the Red House in Lenox with Duyckinck and Mathews, and the following week he delivered to Hawthorne the package sent by Duyckinck in his care, which unknown to him contained all of his own published books. By the time Melville came to stay with the Hawthornes, 3 to 7 September, they had read or reread most of these books and they had also read, though without knowing Melville's authorship, the essay in the *Literary World.* A strong and significant friendship had begun. With the revelation of Melville's authorship of "Hawthorne and his Mosses," which would come by late September, the relationship would be further deepened. There would be more visits, there would be letters exchanged between them. And in November 1851 there would be Melville's next book, *Moby-Dick,* dedicated to Hawthorne.

Of the important settings in the Berkshires for the acquaintance of Melville and Hawthorne first, perhaps, came the houses in which these men lived. By an arrangement made through the friendship of the wives, the Hawthornes lived from May 1850 to November 1851 in a very modest old farmhouse on the William Aspinall Tappan estate, some two miles west of the village of Lenox. To the Red House on the shore of Lake Mahkeenac, commonly called the Stockbridge Bowl, Hawthorne gave the name of Tanglewood, and to the nearby stream the name of Shadowbrook. Here were written *The House of Seven Gables, The Wonder Book,* and parts of *The Blithedale Romance.* Here Melville first called on Hawthorne at home, with Duyckinck and Mathews, 8 August 1850, and Duyckinck commented:

> Hawthorne we found on one of the most purely beautiful spots in the region. His home is a small red farm house but his wife . . . has fitted it up with great taste—particularly a little room or passage or closet or oratory which looks out on the *view*—a fresh rippling lake at the foot of descending meadows, encircled by mountains in the distance—Fine art prints savoring of Italy hung on low walls and a fine engraving of the Transfiguration presented by Emerson.

The view was for Hawthorne a constant source of pleasure and he described it through seasonal changes. In August:

> Monument Mountain, in the early sunshine; its base enveloped in mist, parts of which are floating in the sky, so that the great hill looks really as if it were founded on a cloud. Just emerging from the mist is seen a yellow field of rye, and, above that, forest.

In October:

> The foliage having its autumn hues, Monument Mountain looks like a headless sphinx, wrapped in a rich Persian shawl.

In February:

> The sunsets of winter are incomparably splendid, and when the ground is covered with snow. . . . our southern view . . . with the clouds and atmospherical hues, is quite indescribable and unimaginable; and the various distances of the hills that lie between us and the remote dome of Taconic are brought out with accuracy unattainable in summer.

In May:

> I think the face of nature can never be more beautiful than now. . . . Monument Mountain and its brethren are green, and the lightness of the tint takes away something from their massiveness and ponderosity, and they respond with livelier effect to the shine and shade of the sky.

The road between the Red House and Pittsfield passed through Lenox, the county seat until 1859. In the court house, built in 1816, Chief Justice Lemuel Shaw, Melville's father-in-law, held circuit court nearly every autumn during the early years of Melville's Pittsfield residence. Charles Sedgwick was county clerk from 1821 to 1855; his wife ran an important school for girls; his novelist sister, Catherine Maria Sedgwick, was now a member of his household. Fanny Kemble spent much of her time in Lenox, and had given a clock for the tower of the little white church on the hill, by which Melville and Duyckinck read time driving home by moonlight from the Red House to Arrowhead.

In the summer of 1850 Melville and his wife and year-old son were boarders in Pittsfield at Broadhall, for some years then run as a boarding house by his widowed aunt and cousin Robert Melvill. Longfellow and ex-President John Tyler had stayed there in earlier summers. Here Cornelius Mathews and Evert Duyckinck were installed in August 1850, and the latter wrote to his wife:

> Melville's is a rare place—an old family mansion, wainscoted and stately, with large halls & chimneys—quite a piece of mouldering rural grandeur—The family has gone down & this is their last season. The farm has been sold. Herman Melville knows every stone & tree & will probably make a book of its features.

Built by Henry Van Schaack in 1781, Broadhall had been sold in 1807 to Elkanah Watson, from whom Major Thomas Melvill, Sr., of Boston had bought it in 1816 for his son Thomas Melvill, from 1812 on the U.S. Army Superintendent in Pittsfield, charged with securing supplies during the War of 1812. Melville had frequently visited his uncle's family there during the 1830's, especially in summers, and probably during the fall of 1837, when he taught at the Sykes District school only three miles or less from this house. In October 1850 the house was sold to John R. Morewood and his wife Sarah, but it continued to be the scene of many festive occasions for Melville, for Mrs. Morewood was an inveterate party-giver. Hawthorne was a guest there for dinner 4 September 1850. Still dominant on its eminence south of the center of town, Broadhall has been the Pittsfield Country Club since 1899. The house and setting of Saddle Meadows in *Pierre* were clearly suggested in many features by Broadhall.

When Melville decided, after the summer at Broadhall, to make his home in Pittsfield, he bought 14 September 1850 a farm adjoining Broadhall on the east with an old house built about 1780-1782 by Capt. David Bush and at one time run as an inn by later members of the Bush family. Melville was to live in this house for the next thirteen years, and after the sale to his brother Allan in 1863, he was still frequently a visitor there. The present owner is Mrs. Hale Holden. Melville christened it Arrowhead, because he found arrowheads on the property, as Oliver Wendell Holmes had also found on his grounds only a little way down the road at Canoe Meadows. There were rumors at the time of the purchase that Melville intended to build a larger and more elegant house and to improve the grounds, but the addition of a porch on the north facing the distant Greylock was the only change made. And now the porch has been removed and a picture window framing the mountain view substituted. In Melville's day there was a clear view south to Washington Mountain, as it was called until Melville's name October Mountain stuck. Here Melville lived with his wife, children, mother, and unmarried sisters. As a guest here with his brother in 1851, Evert Duyckinck remarked:

> At the daughter-full house we had a most kind reception. It is an exceedingly pleasant spot, my window now looking out over a miraculous range of meadow and mountain . . . an old improved farm house. . . . The grounds would satisfy an English nobleman—for the noble maples and elms and various seclusions and outlooks and all for the price of a bricked city enclosure of 25 x 100!

Various features of Arrowhead were used by Melville in "The Piazza," "I and My Chimney," and "October Mountain." On a visit here in March 1851, Hawthorne noted the "fine snow-covered prospect of Greylock."

For residents and especially summer visitors to the Berkshires among the chief sights of interest were the Shaker villages at Hancock, four miles west of Pittsfield, and at Mt. Lebanon, just across the line in New York state. In 1776, Mother Anne Lee and her followers had established at Niskayuna, New York, the first American community of Shakers (properly called the Milennial Church or the United Society of Believers in Christ's Second Appearing). They held property in common and they practiced celibacy. By 1850 communities of the sect were scattered from Maine to Kentucky. Hawthorne on a trip to New Hampshire in 1831 with his uncle, Samuel Manning, visited the Shaker community at Canterbury, and half seriously protested interest in becoming a Shaker. "The Canterbury Pilgrims" and "The Shaker Bridal" were literary fruits of this visit. On 28 September 1842, he visited the Shakers at Harvard, Massachusetts, with Emerson, "who had a theological discussion with two of the Shaker brethren."

Melville's earliest known visit to the Hancock Shaker village came 21 July 1850, with his cousin Robert Melvill, when he bought a copy of *A Summary View of the Milennial Church, &c.* He brought his house guests, Duyckinck and Mathews, back to Hancock 7 August 1850. And with the two Duyckincks and Hawthorne, Melville was there again 8 August 1851, when Evert Duyckinck described the visit for his wife:

> Mr Hawthorne had never been. We met them mowing their carefully groomed fields and at the Hancock settlement met again old Father Hilliard and trod the neat quiet avenues whose stillness might be felt. Here is the great circular barn where the winter cattle feed with their heads all to the huge hay mow in the centre. . . . induced venerable Father Hilliard to open to us the big house. Its oiled and polished pine floors were elegant in spite of Shakerdom. The glazed finish of the white walls were as pure as yesterday's work, though they have been there these twenty years. Among these marks of neatness was a small funnel and pipe to carry off the smoke of each lamp to the chimney. A tall old clock stood in the hall but some gay flowers on its face had been covered with white paint. You see no flowers in the sisters' rooms but a volume of unreadable theology (of its kind) with a pair of crossed spectacles by its side on a small table.

From Hawthorne's recorded comments on the same visit it is easy to see that disgust would have kept him from making an excursion to Hancock on his own initiative:

> There were no bathing or washing conveniences in the chambers; but in the entry there was a sink and wash-bowl, where all attempts at purification were to be performed. The fact shows that all their miserable pretence of cleanliness and neatness is the thinnest superficiality; and that the Shakers are and must needs be a filthy set. And then their utter and systematic lack of privacy; the close function of man with man, and supervision of one man over another—it is hateful and disgusting to think of; and the sooner the sect is extinct the better. . . . At the doors of the dwellings, we saw women sewing or otherwise at work; and there seemed to be a kind of comfort among them, but of no higher kind than is enjoyed by their beasts of burden. Also, the women looked pale, and none of the men had a jolly aspect. They are certainly the

> most singular and bedevilled set of people that ever existed in a civilized land. . . .

Mt. Lebanon (the Mother Community in 1850) was also included in Melville's visit of 7 August 1850, but it was more commonly a Sunday attraction. He attended the religious services of the Shakers there with Duyckinck and Mathews 11 August 1850, with Sam Shaw 3 August 1851, and with the Duyckinck brothers 10 August 1851. This last occasion Evert Duyckinck described as

> a ghastly scene. A glass eyed preacher holding forth like an escaped maniac. . . . The audience was very full of city fashionables from Columbian Hall. . . . The dance was long and protracted striking up afresh with new tunes, to the old saw filing, and some of them were profusely jolly. The handshaking accompaniment is ludicrous enough having the appearance of weighing some imaginary groceries in each hand.

Melville's interest was probably more serious than Hawthorne's, though certainly not approving, as attested by his portrait of a Shaker in Gabriel of the Jeroboam in *Moby-Dick*. When Melville set out on a tour of Berkshire county with his cousin Robert (as the official inspector of crops) in July 1850, he purchased a copy of *A History of the County of Berkshire, Massachusetts*, which had been edited in 1829 by David Dudley Field, Sr., father of his Stockbridge host of a few days later. In this volume he marked the passage describing the famous circular stone barn at Hancock, and on the visit to the village he bought, and doubtless read carefully, a volume of Shaker theology.

Perhaps stronger in impact on Hawthorne and Melville than the entertaining excursions to the Shaker villages, or the parties and picnics of the Morewoods, or even than the marshalling of such celebrated conversationalists as the Field dinner in Stockbridge was the effect of nature as revealed in the Berkshires. Hawthorne made repeated journal entries about Monument Mountain as it appeared in the changing season. Melville was impressed by the Balance Rock, a white marble boulder of several tons neatly poised at a point of contact of only a few inches on another, almost completely buried boulder. About a mile north-west of Lake Pontoosuc, then in an open field, the rock was hardly so large as Melville's "huge as a barn" suggests, but it was a popular place for people to carve names and initials. J. E. A. Smith (1879) suggested that it was Melville himself who carved thereon the name "Memnon," and in *Pierre*, as "the Memnon Stone" and "the Terror Stone," it is invoked by the duty-haunted hero as he lies precariously beneath:

> . . . if invisible devils do titter at us when we most nobly strive; if Life be a cheating dream . . . then do thou, Mute Massiveness, fall on me!

Nature, of course, is most impressively represented in the Berkshires by Greylock, that "respectable mountain" Hawthorne noted, coming north from Pittsfield, on his first visit to the county in 1838. Even earlier, the view of Greylock from Broadhall must have impressed the young Melville on visits to his uncle's farm. Strictly speaking, the Greylock range (formerly called Saddle Mountain) is made up of six eminences, which—when seen from the correct angle and distance—are, as Hawthorne said when he viewed them from Vermont, "all mighty, with a mightier chief." The diagram, with the north at the top, indicates the relative locations:

A	Mt. Williams	2951 ft.	A
B	Mt. Prospect	2690 ft.	B
C	Mt. Fitch	3110 ft.	C
D	Stony Ledge	2590 ft.	
	(formerly Bald Mountain)		D
E	Mt. Greylock (formerly Saddleback)		
	has tower on it	3491 ft.	E
F	Saddle Ball	3238 ft.	F

The air-line distance from A to F is perhaps eight miles. Broadhall and Arrowhead are perhaps a dozen or more miles south of F. The level of the surrounding valleys is 600 to 700 feet above sea-level. Thus the main bulk of the mountain towers nearly 3000 feet above Williamstown (roughly three miles north of B) or North Adams (three miles east of A) or Adams (perhaps two miles east of E). Hopper Brook, running northwest from near summit E—with a branch from the north making a declivity between B and C, and a branch from the south making a declivity between D and E, cuts down the center of what is known as the Hopper, because of its resemblance in shape to the hopper of a grist mill. Viewed from Broadhall or Arrowhead, Saddle Ball and Saddleback (or Greylock) appear as twin peaks very much higher than the rest of the mass and vaguely resemble a saddle, for a man riding west. Only at a distance from the east, looking toward Adams (at the foot of E) does Mt. Greylock loom above the mass as a single peak.

At one time or another Melville explored alone or with friends all of this vast mountainous mass, and *Pierre* reflected his intimate knowledge of it. It was clearly in the upper Hopper that he found the amaranth and the catnip in conflict like "man's earthly household peace and the ever-encroaching appetite for God." The once familiar "Delectable Mountain" became in the phantasmagoria of Pierre's vision "the Mount of the Titans." One of "the recumbent sphinx-like shapes thrown off from the rocky steep" above and lying in the upper field of the Hopper near Mt. Fitch Pierre identified with "Enceladus the Titan . . . writhing from out the imprisoning earth;—turbaned with upborne moss." "Young collegian pedestrians," Williams College students no doubt, had excavated some thirteen feet around the statue-boulder, revealing "the turbaned head of igneous rock rising from out the soil, with its unabasable face upturned toward the mountain, and the bull-like neck clearly defined." Imaging the indifference of nature to the fate of man, in the vision Pierre saw "on the Titan's armless trunk, his own duplicate face."

Moby-Dick was dedicated to Hawthorne, "in token of my admiration of his genius," and Melville wrote exultantly to him:

> I feel that the Godhead is broken up like the bread at the Supper, and that we are the pieces. Hence this infinite fraternity of feeling. . . . Knowing you persuades me more than the Bible of our immortality. . . . The divine magnet is on you, and my magnet responds. Which is the biggest? A foolish question—they are *One*.

But Hawthorne had moved away from the Berkshires long before *Pierre* was finished. For "most bounteous and unstinted fertilisations," Melville must now look north from Arrowhead to the mountain. So to that dominating feature of the Berkshires, the author with cheerless bravado dedicated his book, "whether, thereto, The Most Excellent Purple Majesty of Greylock benignantly incline his hoary crown or no."

JEANNE C. HOWES

3. *Melville's Sensitive Years*

IN THE *Sketch of Major Thomas Melvill, Jr. Written by a Nephew* Melville recalls the days of the 1830's which he spent as an adolescent on his uncle's farm in south Pittsfield. Melville's biographers and critics alike agree that his life and writings were strongly influenced by the repeated and extended visits with his uncle's interesting family at Broadhall during those impressionable years. Here he developed a warm and tender feeling for Uncle Thomas and established a secure attachment with the hospitable homestead. Here he learned of the strange sea wanderings of his ex-midshipman cousin, Thomas Wilson Melvill who had once visited Typee valley and who never returned home again from a whaling voyage.

It was during this period, too, that Melville got his start as a writer. Pittsfield was the home of Charles West, a teacher who clearly remembered student Melville's enthusiasm for writing themes—a teacher, incidentally, with a wonderful library and a fondness for the lyrics of Dibdin (Pittsfield *Sun,* July 11, 1889). Here, too, Melville continued his writing apprenticeship while serving as a district schoolmaster, using his leisure for "occasional writting and reading."

These were the days that stirred young Melville's emotions, fired his imagination, and prompted his literary ambitions. This time and place form a vital share of Melville's "visible world of experience . . . that procreative thing which impregnates the muse." (*Pierre*). I thought it therefore highly worthwhile to examine this submerged background by studying the Pittsfield newspapers published during the years of 1833 through 1838. The period indeed has vanished like the "old Elm of the Green", but the record of its events shown in the newspaper columns is preserved for all to see.

Although my extensive perusal of microfilm copies of the *Sun* for the years 1833-38 makes no claim of a comprehensive method or exhaustive research, my copious notes suggest a three-fold value. These old columns not only reveal many interesting facets of the visible world of Pittsfield which influenced Melville's creative growth, but they also served themselves as literary source material to feed his developing imagination. Furthermore, as an opportune outlet for young Melville's early experimental writings, they can be mined for possible nuggets.

At first my attention was focused on the primary sources of Melville's experience—the elm rising 126 feet in the village center, the Berkshire Agricultural Society, the sheep, the crops, the textile manufacturing, Saint Stephen's Episcopal Church, Chief Justice Shaw, the school notices, Edward A. Newton, the post-office, Allen's bookshop, the temperance movement, politics, and Catharine Sedgwick.

In the mass of material, a number of curiously interesting and unrelated items turned up—bits of sermons, patent medicine advertisements, notices of visiting menageries with their train of exotic animals, schedules for Jason Clapp's stage accomodations which Melville undoubtedly used on trips between Pittsfield and Albany, and the description of a bedstead for the sick—"an easy rocking and rolling chair" (Pittsfield *Sun*, Oct. 9, 1834) which could be the original of the invalid's easy chair described in *The Confidence Man.*

Then as parts began to fit together in related wholes, one could piece out the larger fabric of Melville's life in the early Berkshire days—how the annual Cattle Show and Fair dominated and seemed to epitomize every aspect of the village life, how the force of Major Thomas Melvill's complex personality and example influenced an impressionable youth, and how the context of Melville's short-lived teaching career was patterned by a storm of controversy raging about the common schools. We can look at each of these visible remnants in turn.

THE FAIR. The two day Cattle Show and Fair sponsored by the Berkshire Agricultural Society was held on the Pittsfield village green early every October. No other event of Berkshire life received as much or as varied press coverage. Plans were made and announced months in advance; program arrangements carefully detailed and schedules printed at the most useful times; prize winners and contest results posted in full shortly after. But the Fair could serve as a conversation piece any time. The October days were but the climax of a year-long preoccupation, and all the activities encompassed there seemed but a summary of the Berkshire way of life.

Noting that Maria Gansevoort Melville was receiving mail at the Pittsfield post office in early October (*Sun*, Oct. 1, 1834), one may guess that Herman attended the Fair of 1834. Thomas Melvill served that year as chairman in charge of manufactures—both home and factory made. He reported that with the "unpropitious weather" there were only 121 articles presented for examination, mostly cloth and clothing, but also the previously noted "model of a Bedstead for the Sick."

On that occasion the Pittsfield Young Ladies Benevolent Society acknowledged $290 from their Sale in the Lecture Room (Admission 25c—children 12½c) and issued a "Card" publicly thanking "the young gentlemen who aided in the arrangements." Was Herman among them?

Throughout the 1830's the two-day affair followed much the same procedure. The Animal Show was the highlight of the first day. Exhibitors registered at the Town Hall and placed their stock in specially designated pens on the green—oxen in one, cattle in another, a third for sheep, swine and horses, and a fourth for noncompeting animals.

A ploughing match was scheduled the morning of the second day. The Sale and auction were held on both days. Dinner for 50c (Sept. 25, 1834) was served one day at Russell's Hotel and the next at Field's Coffee House. At 11 a.m. on the second day a company of Berkshire Greys led the grand procession from the hotel to the Meeting House for the main address and committee reports. The reverend clergy always shared in the ceremonies with prayers and music.

The Fair of 1835 celebrated its 25th anniversary. The *Sun* reported the ploughing match as a most exciting and noble spectacle. A pair of students from the Medical Institute who had not registered ploughed anyhow and came out first. The grand parade brought an overflow crowd to the Congregational meetinghouse to hear services by Rev. Brinsmaid and the main address by Professor Mark Hopkins who "sustained his high and well earned reputation". Editor Allen also had praise for

> a splendid exhibition of Household Manufactures wrought with your own hands, with the HUM of the Spinning Wheel and the MUSIC of the Grand Piano Forte of Berkshire—the Loom.

Berkshire historians record that the Fair inspired some memorable poems by William Cullen Bryant and Oliver Wendell Holmes. It also loosed several flights of fancy from local literary amateurs. This one (Sept. 29, 1836) offers an apt summary of the occasion.

The Agricultural Fair

Hail! Yeomanry of Berkshire! hail!
Ye hearts of oak to culture given,
Ye whose homes are the hill and dale,
Whose cheerful toils are blest of heav'n,
Come leave for once the teeming fields,
And rest awhile again the plough.
A willing world admiring yields
To you the wealth of honour now.
A day when yeomen far and near
And wives in homespun gown
Bring the fruits of the current year
In rarities to town.
For the first in mechanistic arts
And culture of the soil
Are greeted by Applauding hearts
And Premiums crown their toil.
. . .
And all with philosophic grace
Shall talk their methods o'er
Exchanging doctrines face to face
T'expand their farming lore.
There's a "show" of homemade goods and crops,
Cattle, sheep, horses, swine;
A "Fair" for selling or for *swaps*
As people may incline.
Here's the cow of ample forehead
Graceful neck and polished skin
On the sweet upland pastures fed.
. . .
And yon behold the blooded steed

Whose stately pride the morning mocks
And see from off the rowen mead
Those fair white bleating fleecy flocks.
And ladies bring to public gaze
Their carpets and their woollen stuffs,
Linens, counterpanes, blankets, stays,
Handbags, gloves, hose, mittens, and ruffs.
The gay Hall of Exhibition
Is crowded thus in all its parts
And *belles* may receive tuition
In domestic sciences and arts
Outrement as that of Boarding School
In naughty cities, a la mode,
Where learned of dress the highest rule
And senseless refinements a load.
Here's the rare prize—a wife that knows
A little of domestic cares
Can sew an apron or mend hose
And attend to her "home affairs".
. . .
Behold afar in yonder fields
The hearty Ploughmen strive,
The furrow smokes, the greensward yields
Before the eager drive.

UNCLE THOMAS. The name of Thomas Melvill occurs a number of times in the Pittsfield *Sun* during the years before his departure for Illinois in the summer of 1837. The various items show several facets to delineate a fuller picture of this unusual gentleman.

Something of his earlier role in Pittsfield is preserved in a piece called "Historical Notices, No. 22": "Major Thomas Melville [sic] as Quartermaster and Agent of General Dearborn" had served at the Cantonment with "two buildings for barracks and off quarters, two for stores and a guardhouse where five to six thousand prisoners were kept under a strong guard" before being sent to Montreal. (February 12, 1835).

His spirit of conviviality as well as his political affiliation is shown in a report of toasts he offered at a Democratic Party Supper: "By Thomas Melvill, 4th Vice President,

Our Victories, military and naval—It is not unbecoming a moral and religious people to rejoice at and commemorate them.

The article appearing in the January 14, 1836 edition also repeats another toast he made "to the memory of John Hancock and Samuel Adams", as well as a militant suggestion offered by his son Robert Melvill, all of eighteen, concerning

Our difficulties with France:
If powder must be smelt
Let the ball be felt.

Once in a while Uncle Thomas' name appears on Postmaster Danforth's list of people with mail waiting for them at the post office. Most of the time, however, the name appears in connection with the notices of the Cattle Show and Fair. As "Secretary pro tem" of the Berkshire Agricultural Society, he announced in the *Sun* for March 26, 1835, the contest regulations for the next Fair, and in the fall he headed the list of the Committee on Arrangements. His crop of barley that year was judged second best in the county. At the Fair of 1836, he was honored as "first to introduce the Ruta Baga within the County" and won an award for his crop.

For several years he served as Chairman of Manufactures, examining and awarding prizes for samples of cloth, rugs and coverlids, stockings, mittens, bonnets, stair carpeting, linen sheets and shirting made at home, occasional pieces of cotton or satinett from the Pittsfield mills, and a variety of handmade articles such as Windsor Blinds, Cabinet Work, Dental Instruments and Bedsteads or chairs.

Thomas Melvill contributed more to the Pittsfield *Sun* than the annual list of premium winners. Of greater significance were his anonymous letters which he acknowledged in the issue of October 29, 1835:

. . . the articles in the Pittsfield *Sun* under the signature of Ben Austin were written by me; for them and them only, I hold myself responsible. . . .

Some of the Ben Austin letters opposed the law of imprisonment for debt, some railed against lawyers or attacked members of the opposition party, and others spoke out on the irregular and unjustifiable practices of banks. Their style had a little more bite and color than this sample taken from the truly signed letter quoted above:

> It is not necessary that I should give myself the trouble to reply either to the manner you have introduced my name into your paper or to your inferences and invectives. Your foundation being rotten, your whole superstructure has fallen to the ground: therefore your personal allusions and remarks I leave to an enlightened public. Justice for your outrageous attack on my character will be sought in another tribunal.

These public exchanges with political figures and the editor of the Berkshire *Eagle* bear a striking similarity to the tone and manner of young Melville's later excursions into the columns of the Albany *Microscope* in 1838.

Thomas Melvill's interest and influence in common school education surely played a role in Herman's choice of a teaching career. The pages of the *Sun* reveal some of the uncle's activities as a school committeeman. An ad for April 26, 1837 reads:

> An Instructress Wanted for the South Centre School District. Apply to Thomas Melvill, Prudential Committee.

Letters signed B. A. (Ben Austin) further reveal his feelings and active concern. The following letter (April 13, 1837) is particularly noteworthy not only because it suggests a role for Chief Justice Lemuel Shaw, but because it proposes a County Convention four months in advance of Horace Mann's decision to use this method to launch his crusade for the common schools of Massachusetts.

> Messrs. Allen—Is not the lamentable state of our Common Schools of sufficient importance to warrant the call of a Convention of the County for the purpose of deliberating and acting on the subject? We think so; and therfore suggest the propriety of measures being immediately taken for its meeting during the approaching session of the Supreme Judicial Court. Chief Justice Shaw will be present, whose zeal for the improvement of these institutions and indeed for every measure tending to promote the cause of education is well known.
>
> B. A.

THE COMMON SCHOOL CONTROVERSY. Despite the scarcity of personal source material regarding Melville's teaching career in Pittsfield, a clearer picture of his experience can be obtained by examining its context in the background of the period. It has generally been overlooked that Melville's initiation as a teacher exactly coincided with the launching of the Common School Revival in the fall of 1837 in Berkshire County. The Pittsfield *Sun* of September 21, 1837 confirms that Horace Mann, first Secretary of the Massachusetts Board of Education, delivered an address at the Court House in Lenox on Wednesday, Sept. 13, 1837, to a convention of people interested in the improvement of the county's common schools. The report of this meeting is signed by its chairman, Edward A. Newton.

The name of Newton (which was inadvertently printed as *Norton* in Gilman's account of Melville's early years) is doubly important: first, because he was Mann's bitterest opponent, and second, because he was vividly remembered by Melville.

As a newly appointed teacher Melville should have been in the audience that heard Mann's "eloquent and instructive address." His letter to uncle Peter Gansevoort stated,

> Orators may declaim concerning the universally diffused blessings of education in our Country, and Essayists may . . . extol . . . our sistim of common school instruction, but when reduced to practise, the high and sanguine hopes excited by its imposing appearance in theory—are a little dashed.

Horace Mann was probably one of the orators he had in mind, and the sentence seems to echo the resolutions recorded in Newton's report for the *Sun*:

> *Resolved*, That the Common Schools of the State are among the noblest monuments of the forecast of our fathers, as it regards the general intelligence and the moral elevation of the character of the people.
>
> *Resolved*, That the Common School System is good in theory, inasmuch as it contemplates the education of the whole people, but extremely defective in practical results. . . .

It was in the earlier mentioned *Sketch* of his uncle that Melville recalled Newton as the Major's associate of a Sunday between services at St. Stephen's Episcopal Church. Melville described him as "eminent among the magnates of the village," "a tall stately gentleman" and "well known as a man of fortune who had travelled and who lived with all things handsome about him like the old English Squire in the play." As chairman of the Berkshire County School Association, Edward A. Newton held an influential place in Melville's brief school career.

It was Newton's aristocratic temperament (which Melville clearly recognized) together with his deeply conservative religious strain, that set Newton against Mann. At first they served together on the State Board of Education, but their dislike for each other was soon apparent. In early September 1837, Mann complained to his journal that Newton as head of the Berkshire association had done very little preparation for the County Convention—"if there is not more life in the body than in the head it will soon decompose."

The public break between them came in August 1838, when Mann, who insisted on strict separation between church and school, refused to endorse Sunday school publications suggested by Newton for inclusion in the public school library list. Newton resigned from the State Board and became Mann's lifelong enemy, attacking him for bringing godlessness into the schools.

However, Berkshire County also produced one of Mann's strongest champions—Catharine Maria Sedgwick, who was also known to Melville and his family. Herman's sister Helen attended the private boarding school in Lenox which was directed by Miss Sedgwick's sister-in-law, Mrs. Charles Sedgwick. It is interesting to note that Mrs. Sedgwick and Hope Shaw came to visit the Melvill home in Pittsfield in the fall of 1837. Elizabeth Shaw, Helen's very close friend, was probably also enrolled at Mrs. Sedgwick's school.

Catharine Sedgwick was a very popular author of the time whose books Mann did approve of for public school reading. An item in the *Sun* for Dec. 27, 1836 indicates that Miss Sedgwick was interested in preparing a textbook to be used in the common schools. The information occurs in a public letter to J. Orville Taylor, the Albany educationist whose book on district schools Melville would review a year later for Uncle Peter. Miss Sedgwick, apparently at Taylor's suggestion, agreed to prepare a *Class Book for Girls*, "a reading book" which she "will undertake with pleasure" but "cannot promise to have it done in less than a year." Her faith in the educability of those who cannot afford private schooling is clear:

> It will go into the hands of precisely that class of persons that I am most desirous of benefitting and which I consider most teachable.

The next school convention Mann attended in Berkshire was held in Pittsfield on September 17, 1838. The account reported in the *Sun* states that Edward Newton was chairman for the meeting and Charles Sedgwick secretary; no mention is made of Catharine Sedgwick. Mann's journal, however, singles her out as one of the few who appreciated and supported his stand at what must have been a very controversial meeting. Mann deplores the small attendance, but the *Sun* speaks of "a very large and respectable audience".

It is possible that Melville was present at this meeting for he was very likely in town for the wedding of his cousin Robert Melvill to Miss Susan Bates that same evening. By that date, however, if Herman's career as a district school master wasn't already over, it was rapidly coming to an end.

Inasmuch as Herman Melville was personally acquainted with the Berkshire personalities involved in the stormy school controversy, he could not help but be deeply aware of the ideological clash and its tremendous implications.

LITERARY SOURCE MATERIAL. It seems only reasonable to assume that Melville read these issues of the Pittsfield *Sun*. Uncle Thomas, a literate man and occasional contributor to its columns, was undoubtedly a regular subscriber. In those days newspapers were not hastily discarded but carefully kept for future reference and repeated readings. Any one familiar with Melville's reading habits must believe that he read all he could lay his hands on. To Melville, as Jay Leyda claims, the reading of books and newspapers was as vivid as direct personal participation in an experience, and pictures stirred him as deeply as print.

The *Sun* therefore offers more than a firsthand context of Pittsfield life during Melville's adolescence: the words, ideas and images appearing in these pages nourished Melville's imagination during the formative years. In addition to regular coverage of national and state affairs, there are local notices and advertisements, paragraphs of practical information, comments on curiosities, weather conditions, agricultural methods, fashion notes, church and missionary news and legal announcements. Every issue carried a literary column featuring poetry often reprinted from such places as the *Knickerbocker Magazine,* the New York *Mirror* or Boston or Albany papers. Some of the literary products were contributed locally and some were anonymous. Here are the sentimental lines of Mrs. Hemans, verses by Whittier, many poems by Bryant, and frequently a piece by the very popular Nathaniel Parker Willis.

The Allen bookstore was quick to announce every new Willis publication for sale—*Melanie and Other Poems,* the English edition of *Poems of N. P. Willis* edited by Barry Cornwall, and *Inklings of Adventure.* In one review Allen wrote, "The great and free land of America must of necessity produce great poets and eminent men" and he listed "Cooper, Brockden Brown, Washington Irving, Miss Sedgwick, Bryant, Halleck and Willis" as candidates in the field.

Among the Willis pieces that appeared in the *Sun* were excerpts from *First Impressions or Notes by the Way,* an account of the Grand Bazaar of Constantinople (Nov. 20, 1834) and a "Passage from Edith Linsley in *Inklings,* plus such poems as May" (Aug. 18, 1836), "Lines for a Two Year Old", and "Lines on Leaving Europe" (Mar. 9, 1837), also brief paragraphs like this one:

> Nature: To a man of deep emotion, nature is a mirror full of shifting images, to an unmoved one, only a window through which he sees what is going on around him.

Factual and descriptive information about the region appeared in a series of "Historical Notices" No. 1 through No. 22, printed throughout 1833 and 1834, and in the form of local legends. The "Notices" traced back the origins of the town and reviewed its present conditions, its roads, shops, schools, and churches. One of the legends called "Indian Traditions of Monument Mountain" suggests the mountain scenes of *Pierre* and the picturesque style of *Typee* in these passages:

> If there is anything sublime attached to a mount, a rare beauty will be admitted to linger around this wild and towering line of rocks. Its bold and frowning front extends one mile. . . . A few knotty dwarfish pines are to be seen peering obliquely from the narrow crevices. . . . The red bolt from the thunderclouds, the winds, and the power of centuries, have torn away many

fragments of stone from on high and sent them smoking to the base. . . .

Below all was in miniature—the rocks were dwindled to a level with the surrounding vale, the trees had shrunk away to bushes, and an old chief who was sitting on a rock stringing a bow was but a speck and the outline of his form could scarcely be traced. . . .

It was on the night of the second day . . . the sun fell away at eve with a peculiar splendor turning every object in the valley to a golden light, and causing the Housatonic in its serpentine course to gleam up and spangle like liquid fire. . . . Night had set in with all its blackness, a flame of fire suddenly lit up the world, the pine was struck by a thunderbolt, setting it on fire, which being parted from the cleft of the rock, spun round and round. . . . Upward it hurried into the air, burning and whizzing in its course, the torrents of rain not even dimming its glare. (October 31, 1833)

William Pitt Palmer who was attending classes at the Berkshire Medical Institute at this time had a talent for writing poetry. In 1834 an ode of his was sung by the Temperance Society at the Lecture Room. Its theme and imagery could have suggested ideas for *Mardi* or "The Enviable Isles." It was published in the Nov. 6, 1834 edition:

O! soft sleep the hills in their sunny repose,
In the lands of the South where the vine gaily grows
And blithesome the hearts of the vintagers be
In the grape-purpled vales in the isles of the sea.
. . . (several verses)
Then lift not the wine-cup—though Pleasure may swim
Like an angel of light round its roseate brim.
Yet dark in the depths of its fountain below
Lurk the Spirits that lure to the vortex of woe!

Another local poet signing himself "J. W." in a poem called "Incense of the Heart" (Dec. 3, 1835) offers a bolder imagery which would also have appealed to Melville:

What is that atom, afar in the sky
In the blaze of the red sun's burning eye,
Wheeling and circling that tenantless air

As though he were tethered returnlessly there?
Like a planet that swims in that other sea
Held in its orbit by destiny
'Tis a rock-nursed eagle; spurning the earth
Darting away from the land of his birth
He quits the low scenes that would trammel him there
To muff the pure gale of that far atmosphere,
He has caught some few rays of that fair sun on high
And unblushingly gazes that sun in his eye.
To thy knees child of Adam—tho' splendor is there
Sublimer yet still is the incense of prayer.

WHALES. Of special interest to any Melville fan are the many references in these pages of the *Sun* to the ocean, ships, and whales. Every issue of the paper carried a woodcut of a whale to advertise sperm oil and sperm candles. Buel and Colt's cut for Nov. 28, 1833 is rather crude compared to the dashing figure of a whale used in the later ads of A. C. Mitchell and Company's sperm oil factory (Sept. 21, 1837). A paragraph for Nov. 16, 1833 describes the "Temperance Lamp" using a mixture of alcohol and spirits of turpentine with the comment, "Surely the *whales* ought to be in favor of this lamp."

In April of 1835 a reprint from the Gloucester *Democrat* spoke of a "Sea Serpent" seen off Race Point Light, Cape Cod. In July of that year a column called "Power of the Swordfish" told how "the brig Fortune was struck abaft the bulkhead by a swordfish which penetrated heavy copper and oak planks."

A paragraph on "Whales" on March 2, 1837 stated:

> A single stroke from the tail of a whale will cut a boat in two—and they move in the sea above a mile a minute. The females are most affectionate to their young and when assailed and wounded by the avaricious monsters who frequent their seas, their care of their young ones often draws tears from every eye witness who is not capable of midnight murder.

A news item for June 5, 1837 tells how the last five whalers brought to port at Stonington returned with more oil and whalebone than any "five successive ships since the business began," and on August 31 that year it was stated, with figures for 1836,

> The value of the whale fisheries is but little understood, and

the rapidity with which their importance has increased still less known.

Details of "A Whale Fight" were reprinted from the New Bedford *Gazette* in the June 1, 1837 copy of the *Sun*:

> A lone male turns on the male leader of females and gives battle bold and destructive. They run backwards from each other several rods, then rapidly advance head foremost, their great square heads meeting with dreadful suddenness. The scene is one of awful display. Two monsters advanced with jaws measuring sixteen feet in length, widely extended, exhibiting huge rows of great teeth presenting a most ferocious appearance. One jaw is broken off and hanging by the flesh, the other with teeth stove in. The conqueror joins the females and resumes the cruise.

A long, humorous piece of verse, reprinted from *Tait's Magazine*, appeared in the *Sun* for Nov. 24, 1836:

Ode To The American Sea Serpent

The monstrous crocodile
The Eldon of the Nile
That hypocritically cries
O'er the devoted prey he draws
Within the Chancery of his jaws—
Whose huge dimensions learned folks discuss
Describing him a *living omnibus*!
(By which if thou'rt inclined to ride
Pray book a place for me—but not inside!)
Though he is, certes, of a monstrous size,
He's but a shrimp to thee
Terrific serpent of the sea!

The broad baleena whale
Is not a patch upon thy tail!
(Which puts great Dan O'Connell's out of joint
And sages say exactly tallies
With that of the great comet, ycleped Halley's;
But this I say is a disputed point.)
Nay e'en the Kraken vast—
Which grave l'ontoppidian, Norwegian bishop

Serves to his readers, as a curious dish up
Would scarce suffice to break thy fast.

The total ocean brine
To thee is but a tiny Serpentine!
Wherein thy facile folds lie sometime curld
Stupendous Python that can clasp the world!
Tis said—and we may well believe
Thou art the serpent that first tempted Eve,
In Eden's fair primeval bower;
Whence driven to the sea for the dread crime
Thou hast been growing ever since *that time*
And now with matchless bulk, astoundest ours!

When stretch'd at length—tis rather droll—
Thy tail doth touch the South
Whilst with thy pointed mouth
Thou breath'st the bracing air of the North Pole
But when thou turn'st the student of Mercator
Beholds a very palpable equator,
And shouldst thou listless on the waves recline
Seamen perceive thee from the mast
And cry "avast!
Yonder's the equinoctial line!"

Then to pursue their voyage at a loss, they
Are somewhat disinclined to *cross* thee!
And if thou mov'st, their terrors don't diminish,
How do they tremble at thy rising *mane*,
Great mayor of ocean
Who, when thou makst a *motion*
Are sure to carry it, 'tis plain!
And when thou showst a fin—they fear a fin-ish!

When sick of salt and water thou on high
Rearest thy awful head towards the sky,
Thy tail beneath the billows and thy spout
Touching the clouds—thou seemst a water-spout!
And while thy stomach disembogueth the seas
The distant steersman trembling at the helm
Fearing the deluge may his bark o'erwhelm
Swift tacks about and from the danger flees.

Farewell! A long farewell!
For I
Have other smaller fish to fry;
Yet this in truth I tell—
Respectfully I bid thee a goodby.
Constrain'd am I to end my song,
Which else must fail;
For thou art a theme *so long*
Although enough I've said
Upon that head
'Tis clear I never can complete thy tale!

A WRITER'S OUTLET. Vincent, who prepared the first American edition of Melville's collected poems, has suggested that the account of Pierre's youthful writings in Melville's *Pierre* may actually allude to early pieces written by the author himself between 1835 and 1840. If such pieces do exist "hidden in magazines under strange pseudonyms" the Pittsfield *Sun* would have been a very likely place for their publication. "The Tropical Summer" never turned up, but there was a little verse called "The Tear" printed anonymously Jan. 21, 1836:

Sweet tribute of the parting hour
Twin sister of the word farewell,
Thy honied nectar has a power
Beyond what human tongues can tell.

Other possible suspects could be "Viator," whose poems were sometimes reprinted from the Albany *Argus*, "T. K. Hervey" or "James G. Percival". Recalling Melville's reference to "the eminent Mr. Roscoe, the historian, poet, and banker," an acquaintance of Redburn's father, in *Redburn*, one pauses over this poem "From a Volume entitled 'Poems for Youth by a Family Circle' supposed to be the product of Mr. Roscoe's family, Liverpool" (Nov. 16, 1833):

I'll be a fairy and drink the dew
And creep through the honied flowers,
And sleep in the violet's tender blue,
And dance in the evening hours.

Remembering, too, Melville's enthusiasm for Camoens in *White Jacket*, this also bears observation (Jan. 29, 1835):

Sonnet—From the Portugese of Camoens
By R. H. Wilde of Georgia
Sonnet xliii of the edition of 1779-1780

They say the Swan though mute his whole life long
Pours forth sweet melody when life is flying.

Is it for life and pleasure past his sighing?
Grieving to lose what none can e'er prolong?
Oh no! He hails its close on death relying.

If indeed Melville's early poems are there, they are too well hidden to be clearly identified. A blessing, surely, if they were as saccharine as Pierre's remembrance of them.

A careful look at the anonymous prose pieces, however, seemed to present better prospects. In the paper for July 23, 1835, the story of Midshipman Wilson seems to have a strong relation to events in the life of ex-midshipman T. Wilson Melvill, the lost cousin. A series called "The Philosopher," items No. 1 through No. 4 of which appeared in the April and May, 1836 issues, seems to reflect some of Melville's early thoughts on education. The pieces were signed "Self Education" and "Mutual Instruction".

Another item one might consider as an early Melville production appears in the *Sun* for June 29, 1837, and is titled "Dangerous Hoax". It relates the story of Mr. D. from Maryland who while on board ship decided to dress as an Indian chief—Powel or Osceola—"the devil incarnate." A crowd on shore hearing the news when the ship docked came aboard to see the illustrious tattoed chief.

> . . . one fellow less credulous than the rest had the curiosity to peep under his robe to see if there was any white skin beneath. I know not what discovery he made, but the report got aboard that the whole was a hoax. This enraged the inhabitants of Vicksburgh (which by the way should have been christened Lynchburg) and they began to shew symptoms of *tar and featherism.* But the friends of D stood by him to a man; each drew a terrific Bowie knife and defied the mob. As the *canaille* always quail before any exhibition of strength and courage they gradually slunk away; and the noble chieftain had leisure to change his "outward man" so effectually that he might have deceived the lynx eye of the omniscient Vidocq himself.

My favorite candidate, however, for a genuine piece of Melville juvenilia, was published in the *Sun* for Sept. 25, 1834—a column called "Autumn" from which these lines are selected:

> In France and Italy they paint him like a Bacchus, crowned with grapes and vine leaves, but that is none of our autumn. He is a plain gentleman farmer, and partakes of no potations, unless perhaps a glass of cider fresh from the press; but this year he will dispense with even that indulgence.
>
> I fancy I see him in the orchard, strolling under the trees with his hands behind him under the broad skirts of his old blue coat, like my reverend uncle from the south, looking thro' his golden rimmed spectacles to catch a glimpse of the apples, peaches and pears among the boughs. He can detect none, however, for they are all gone! They are nipt in the early summer. He walks down to the creek or river, under the shell bark hickories and looks up at their high tops, but he can see no nuts, among the hazle bushes no clusters. . . . Had it been Winter he would have raved, had it been Spring she would have wept, had it been Summer she would have fainted. Autumn never cares, he turns up the lane with his hands still beneath his empty pockets, humming a tune and looking as pleasant as ever.
>
> Passing the cornfield, he climbs over the fence. He looks at the pumpkins turned up to the sun and lays his hands on their green round bellies when they grow golden. Not Midas himself could have gilded them better. As he walks along the rows he touches the silks, as they peep out from the tops of the ears, when, tho' unseen, they become colored like locks of every hue, from the flaxen to the auburn, but most are sandy like his own bright hair.

It is my conclusion that this is an earlier "Sketch" of Major Thomas Melvill written by a devoted nephew. Here is the farmer uncle of Pittsfield examining the returns of his orchard and fields—an uncle with a touch of elegance despite the empty pockets of his old blue coat—an uncle who could keep good-humoured despite the failure of his fruit crop—an uncle who was a kind of a wizard with the simple vegetables of corn and pumpkins.

From this bare factual outline we can move out to identify the specific Melville touches by comparing this simple portrait with the later writings based on or inspired by Melville's concept of his uncle. Before we check with the "Sketch" which is the fullest and finest example, we should glance over a poem called "Trophies of Peace" and the story of "Jimmy Rose".

The poem's subtitle "Illinois in 1840" immediately associates it with Uncle Thomas and the trip Herman made to visit his uncle that summer. The skill and artistry of the poem suggests it was written much later—following the Civil War perhaps—while Melville was finishing up his *Battle-Pieces*. Just as so many of those poems commemorated the lives of the fallen soldiers, so does this verse stand as a memorial to his dead uncle. In these verses the symbol of the golden corn speaks of a serenity and productivity that triumphed over the hostility of life. The poem reflects the same equanimity as the uncle of the "Autumn" piece, and the "silks" described there so vividly are now heightened to a great poetic image. Significantly, the poem is also a harvest symbol.

Behind the transparency of "Jimmy Rose" lies Melville's fictionalized portrait of the urbane, not the rural, Uncle Thomas. Like the uncle of "Autumn" here is a figure in a "thin, threadbare, careful coat", with an elegant style despite his poverty, mild-mannered despite reverses, able to adapt to misfortune philosophically and to make the best of the humble things left.

The factual prose "Sketch" of the Major, however, most clearly shows the identity with the anonymous piece in the Pittsfield *Sun*. We recognize the same basic outline—his activity as a farmer, his pennilessness, his kindly manners and insouciance. But the specific details are unmistakable. The later recollection turns up many of the same associations—the autumn setting, the observer in the field, the plain clothing, the elegant prop—a snuffbox rather than the goldrimmed spectacles. Both pieces mention the acceptance of temperance customs—the closed decanters and the denial of cider. Another striking similarity between the two is the way both of them contrast the ornateness of Europe with the simple American ways.

For me, however, the telling stroke—the Melville fingerprint if you will—can be discerned in the uniquely developed imagery. Although embellished and refined in the later description the essence is fundamentally the same:

> It was the French graft upon the New England stock, which produced this autumnal apple; perhaps the mellower for the frost.

For Melville, Uncle Thomas—patron of the October fair—would remain the personification of the autumn season.

MORSE PECKHAM

4. *Hawthorne and Melville as European Authors*

THE PROBLEM of the culture of the United States is so perplexing and the place in it of the artist and intellectual so baffling, that anyone who attempts to discuss Melville and Hawthorne, if he is not an Americanist, must commit himself to unequivocal statements of his position. That there is an American culture in the sense that there is a European culture and that the problem is one of the interrelation between two independent cultures is to me untenable. Perhaps the position is held by no one, yet I have gathered a different impression. The culture of the United States, then, is neither more nor less than a geographical extension of European culture, and is thus similar to the other cultures of this hemisphere and of the geographical borders of Europe itself—Russia, for example, and Norway.

But I find equally untenable the notion that ours is a provincial culture. Modern Denmark and Sweden, modern Ireland and Spain, are truly provincial; but it is clear to me that though the term "provincial" may properly be applied to Irving and Cooper, it is hopelessly inadequate for Emerson, Hawthorne, Melville, or Emily Dickinson, or Whitman. For such figures some other term is necessary, and we do not have one. Or it may be perfectly accurate to class them as European writers. Nevertheless, they did not live in or write from or for a truly European situation, though they came to live at the highest level of European culture. They were in a situation novel in recent European cultural history. It was the frontier of a geographical extension of an old and highly developed culture of many levels. For the moment let us accept the judgment of the highest cultural level of Europe and assert that the Americanization of European culture is a vulgarization. But let no European assume airs of superiority. It cannot be too strongly asserted that Americanized Europe is more vulgar—a term I hope to give a somewhat more exact meaning to—than the United States. Miami Beach may be a vulgarization of the aristocratic resort of nineteenth-century Europe, but Torremolinos is a more vulgar Miami Beach. In this circumstance lies, I propose, a clue to the problem of the artist and intellectual in the United States.

I should like to call anthropology and psychology to my aid. Everyone knows that when a higher culture encounters a less-developed one, the effect on the latter is disastrous. Yet I have never seen it proposed that when a higher culture is extended to a geographical environment different from that to which its behavioral patterns are adapted, and that when, at the same time, it is exposed to less-developed cultures, a deterioration of its higher cultural levels may, and perhaps must, follow. Yet such I believe to be the case.

The history of the United States is the history of the progressive westward movement of European culture into alien physical environments and in constant contact with less-developed cultures, both Indian and Negro. Thus European culture was transformed into a frontier culture. Frontier patterns are still the basic cultural patterns of the United States, and the frontier values are still our fundamental values. These are scarcely novel propositions, but it seems to me that what a frontier culture involves has not been adequately considered. The highest level of any culture is marked, first, by extreme richness; it contains in solution innumerable ambiguities and ambivalences and puzzles and problems. Anyone who lives at that level is as much involved in discovering and creating problems as he is in solving them. Second, therefore, the life of the members of that highest cultural level requires psychic insulation, for only that makes problem exposure tolerable. Third, that level maintains itself by alliance with political power, social status, and wealth. These are the economic and social defenses for its psychic insulation. The American academic tenure system is an example, though perhaps a rather crude one. Yet it brings out a fourth character of high-level culture; it is exceedingly wasteful in every possible way, from economic to psychic. It must be; the human capacity for problem exposure and controlled innovation is so limited that a tremendous loss is involved in any genuinely high culture creative breakthrough. Parsons College is a financial success because it has eliminated the waste of high culture.

Of course there is no such thing as a culture or a society. There is only the behavior of an infinitude of human beings, none of whom can learn perfectly any cultural pattern. Few have the capacity for high level problem tolerance, even fewer have the capacity for significant creativity, and far fewer have the opportunity for either. It must always be remembered that the highest cultural level exists only because a few people need it in order to adapt to their physical and social environments. This need is mysterious, but a crude explanation is possible.

To me the most significant and useful current theory of cognition is the perceptual or cognitive model theory, sometimes called set theory, or expectancy theory. It is the basis of my recent study of artistic behavior, *Man's Rage for Chaos.* Briefly, it amounts to this: To every situation we bring, by picking up clues from the situation, a perceptual, or cognitive model, or orientation. But since this model is prepared to deal only with a category of situations, but with no existential situation, there is a necessary disparity between the model and the data fed into the brain by the sensorium. That disparity is reality. Our general tendency is to suppress as much of it as possible, because any awareness of it is cognitively disorienting and emotionally disturbing. The safer, the more protected, the human organism, the more it can afford to be aware of disparities, to search for problems, to account for the disparity, to solve those problems, and to correct the original cognitive model by feedback. If the organism does not have to act for its own defense and survival, it can thus become aware both of the disparity between model and sensory data and of difficulties, ambiguities, ambivalences, puzzles in the cognitive models themselves. In a crisis situation, one which it interprets as requiring action, it cannot afford such luxuries. Behavior in crisis situations is, thus, invariably simplistic. A life-history which involves continuous exposure to crisis situations effects an increasing simplification of behavior and a continuous reinforcement of increasingly simplified cognitive models.

A frontier is a crisis situation. Although there are exceptions, all of them technological, the tendency of Europeans on the American frontier, whether North or South America, was necessarily to apply European cognitive models by simplification, reductionism, and reinforcement, rather than by feedback and correction. Instances are easy to come by. In Europe violence, though certainly present, tended to be ritualized, at least in those areas of violence, such as war, under some control by higher cultural levels. But violence on the frontier is the response of the individual who cannot afford the luxury of correcting his adaptational models, but can only apply them by eliminating any disparity from the environment, not by understanding it. Hence our Civil War was the bloodiest war in the history of European culture. Grant's determination to destroy the enemy army and his indifference to elegant manoeuvre and the ritualistic capture of the enemy capital is an instance of frontier, or crisis, behavior—the de-ritualization and hence simplification of cultural patterns. Thus unritualized violence has become endemic to American culture. Whether or not President Kennedy was assassinated by a plot, every American is quite ready to believe that it was the work of an unaided individual; this country is full of trigger-happy crack-pots. But the European is convinced that there must have been a plot, an elaborate behavioral pattern. In the same way, although Enlightenment thinking at its best was very rich, the founding documents of this Republic are almost parodic simplifications of Enlightenment philosophy. Again, as a total behavior pattern, Jackson Pollock's version of European abstract painting was a striking simplification, involving a minimally corrected, rapid, and violent attack upon ever larger canvasses.

But this simplification, reductionism, and reinforcement of behavioral patterns, which to the man at the highest cultural level constitutes vulgarity, had two further consequences, one flowing from the other. The first is that the process was necessarily seen as good. Since it was necessary for survival on the frontier, it was, as values always are, universalized. It was interpreted as an ennoblement, a redemption of, European culture. Here is the source of the myth of America as a Paradise, in spite of all evidence to the contrary, and of the absurd myth of the American as the new Adam. The result was a culture in which behavioral simplification became the ideal. Here is the source of the anti-intellectualism of American life. But the second consequence, flowing from the first, has meant a peculiar American helplessness before the enormous social problems industrialization and uncorrected exploitation of natural and human resources have brought into being. The automobile has destroyed the old semi-rural American culture from which I learned that the only significant human distinction is that of the philosopher, the scientist, and the artist; it has stabbed our cities to the bone; it has polluted our air; and it is killing us at a greater rate than all our wars, just as murder is. We are helpless before it. And we are helpless before the problem of the Negro. It is evident that the efforts of the past ten years have only made the problem worse. Every year fewer white Americans are sympathetic with the Negro's cause, and as an American of almost as many Anglo-Saxon generations in this country as possible, I feel in my bones that millions of my fellow citizens are getting ready to act out what they dream of, the elimination of the problem by the bloody elimination of the Negro.

Nevertheless, as I suggested earlier, let no European feel superior. All this—simplification, idealization of that simplification, helplessness before modern problems—has been exported to Europe and has found there a welcome and an intensification. World War I imitated the American Civil War; the ritualization of European war disintegrated and led to a military process which the Europeans were quite unable to stop, although previously there had been effective patterns for stopping wars. The English have been even more helpless than we in the face of a far less severe Negro problem. Apparently Europeans are incapable of learning from American failures. Experiencing for the first time the onslaught of the automobile, they are proving even more helpless than we have been, for they have far more to be destroyed. If Jackson Pollock made a parodic simplification of Picasso, European artists have made a parodic simplification of Jackson Pollock. If we have pointless riots in Watts and Berkeley, the Europeans have more pointless riots in Amsterdam and West Berlin, simplifications of their consciously imitated American models. But enough; anyone, once alerted, can think of a thousand instances.

Why should this be so? Here it is useful to introduce the notion of the internal frontier. I mean by this the exposure of lower cultural levels to higher. When a man from the middle or lowest cultural level encounters a higher cultural level, he has several strategies at his disposal. He can see that the high level offers what he needs, and if the social situation permits it, he can earn his place there and achieve acceptance. In this sense, European culture has generally been democratic. Or he can retreat back to his own culture, realizing that that is where he properly belongs. Or he can resent his exclusion and demand simplification, reduction, and reinforcement, insisting that the high culture be transformed downward to meet his needs, or what he feels to be his needs. If he has enough political, social, and economic power, he can make his demands felt and acted upon. He can dismantle the high culture. It need only be remembered that exactly the same cognitive forces are at work on the internal frontier as on the external. In the past couple of hundred years those forces have become not only effective in Europe but predominant.

The first factor in the situation was the Enlightenment itself, which was a simplification of European culture at the highest level. It was, to be sure, soon followed by Romanticism, which made that level of culture richer than ever—more ambiguous, ambivalent, self-conscious, and problem and reality oriented. However, in the nineteenth century the most important cultural phenomenon quantitatively was the spread of Enlightenment ideas. But those ideas suffered a further simplification as a consequence of the communications revolution and the enormous increase in literacy and education. For the first time, the whole middle level of culture developed an extremely sensitive awareness of the existence of high culture, and much of this awareness penetrated to the lower levels. Simplification, idealization of simplification, violence, and helplessness were the result. Further, the economic rewards for culture businesses in vulgarizing high culture, particularly publishing, proved to be infinitely greater than in serving it. Inferior culture began to drive superior culture out of the marketplace, making high culture even more dependent on political and economic power. Moreover, one of the direct consequences of Enlightenment thinking was that for members of the high cultural level to vulgarize their own culture was not only safe but a moral imperative. A social environment was created, therefore, in which exposure to American cultural simplifications met not merely acceptance but intensification. This is what I mean, then, when I propose that geographical extension and contact with less-developed societies bring about the deterioration of the high culture of the more developed society. On the internal frontier there is always a demand and a market for the vulgarizations necessarily developed on the external frontier. The deterioration of social support for high culture follows.

From this point of view it is possible to understand the peculiar difficulty of the artist and intellectual in the United States. Since he was one of those people who turned to the highest level of culture because he needed it, he had to turn to the highest level of European culture. There was no other possibility. Any cultural pattern, however, is learned by imitation of a behavioral paradigm. I mean by this that the learning of the behavior patterns of a high culture is not merely learning what can be absorbed from books. It is a matter of learning elaborate behavioral patterns of which published verbal behavior is only a part. In particular, the various techniques for achieving psychic insulation can be learned only paradigmatically. The difficulties of Hawthorne and Melville in learning the necessity for psychic insulation and in improvising insulatory techniques are too well-known to need comment. Such behavior paradigms were by no means absent, but they seem to have been more common in the eighteenth century than in the nineteenth. The carriers of the paradigms had come directly from Europe, and the frontier simplification had not yet much affected them. For instance, as a relatively trivial example, it is known that the exquisite plasterwork in eighteenth-century Philadelphia houses was done by Irish craftsmen who had learned their trade in Dublin.

But the greatest difficulty for the nineteenth-century artist and intellectual, not to speak of the twentieth, was that he was attempting cultural complexity in a situation in which cultural simplification had become the ideal. And so seductive is such an idealization, as in the earlier books of Melville, that it was easy for him to think that somehow there was something wrong about his desire to enter into a world of ambiguity, ambivalence, and exposure to the problems and recalcitrance of reality. Romanticism involves alienation and social isolation, but these were doubled when the American Romantic found himself in a social environment increasingly dominated by the values emerging from the cognitive crisis of the frontier. This is why today's European artist and intellectual believes that some Americans preceded him in the Existential experience. He is partly mistaken, of course. The Existential vision develops out of his own Romantic tradition; it is the modern form of it. But he is right in thinking that the American artist somehow felt its full intensity before the European. That intensity, however, comes not from the character of Existential thinking but rather from the fact that Romanticism historically coincided with the American deterioration of European high-level culture. I should say that, generally speaking, the European scarcely yet knows that the same thing is happening to him. And it needs to be pointed out that he too is feeling the seductiveness of frontier simplification and reinforcement and the consequent helplessness and violence.

For the American intellectual and artist, the only counter-attraction to that simplistic seduction has been Europe itself. Not only was it the source of that high culture which he needed, but it was there that social support for that culture was present. Paradigms existed in numbers enough to make a difference, and they were protected by power, status, and wealth. Hence the climactic experience for the American has been the first visit to Europe. To be sure, actual contact with European high-level culture has usually been a disappointment. The principal reason, perhaps, is that he has not entered the high culture by the paths ritualized in Europe, nor is he familiar by living example with the paradigms. To the European, therefore, he does not properly belong and his pretensions to belong are usually not taken very seriously. For this attitude of the European there is some justification. What American intellectual has not felt bitterly the inadequacies and unnecessarily slow pace of his formal education? Nevertheless, the American learns something of great value, particularly because of his exclusion from the circles he wishes to enter, but also because of the barriers of the most trivial, as well as the most important, language and behavior differentia. He learns that to be what he wants to be he has to be a foreigner in his own country. Whether he lives the rest of his life abroad or at home, the American intellectual who has been to Europe is an expatriate. For even at home, he is a foreigner in a country all of the values of which are aimed in a direction diametrically opposite to the values he desires. For these reasons, therefore, I think it is useful, and perhaps correct, to think of Hawthorne and Melville as European writers.

II

In what follows I should like to propose that these two writers can best be understood as European Romantics. That is, although they often concerned themselves with problems of the United States, the instruments or cognitive models they employed were the same as those of European Romanticism. Further, I wish to propose that their intellectual and artistic development can be understood, and best understood, as recapitulations, more or less independent, of the development of the cognitive models of European Romanticism. To explain this I fear it is first necessary to present here as briefly as I can the main outlines of a theory of Romanticism I have presented elsewhere, though I shall offer some novel propositions. [See my *Beyond the Tragic Vision*, New York, 1962 and *Romanticism: The Culture of the Nineteenth Century*, New York, 1965].

Using again the theory of the cognitive model, it may be said that human organisms experience two difficulties with it. One, insufficient feedback, I have already touched in suggesting that frontier culture is a crisis culture. The other may be called cognitive overload; that is, feedback is too great for the individual to endure. The cognitive model, instead of being corrected, collapses. Studies of creativity have shown that a major creative breakthrough is usually preceded by a disorientation so severe that it resembles psychosis, and is likewise frequently followed by something very like it. My notion of Negative Romanticism is supported by this discovery. That is, the breakdown of Enlightenment thinking through its own internal contradictions and its empirical failure led, in some people at least, to a severe dislocation, or disorientation. This was signified by guilt, alienation, isolation, and wandering: the disappearance of goals and the breakdown of goal-directed activity. The sense of the value of human existence appears only when the individual's cognitive models are instrumentally functional in goal-directed behavior.

The creative breakthrough into Positive Romanticism, or Romanticism proper, was made possible by a new metaphysical insight, quite different from anything that had happened in Europe before. Instead of striving to create a new constitutive metaphysic, or regnant cognitive model, the Romantic created a metaphysic the heart of which was an explanation for the necessity for metaphysics. He looked at himself from right angles, and his fundamental postulate became the Self, or the Subject. Instead of creating a new metaphysic from which the Soul might be derived, he created the Self, the sense of identity, of value, of goal-directed behavior in the service of which any metaphysic exists. But he was not solipsistic. For the Object was as real as the Subject; the categories of neither could exhaust the attributes of the other. Romantic reality thus became the tension, forever unresolveable, between the Subject and Object. Hegel called that tension the Idea, and in this mode of thinking reality is the Idea.

In the course of the nineteenth century, I believe, there emerged four main stages in Romantic development. The first I have called Analogism. It is the stage of Wordsworth and Emerson's *Nature.* The structure and the value of Subject and Object are conceived of as analogous, not identical. Thus the Subject can know that the Object has structure and value, but the nature of that structure and value he cannot know. This solution, however, proved unviable, because it provided no basis either for action or decision. The next stage, which I have called Transcendentalism, solves that problem by conceiving the Object as without structure and value and the task of the Subject as the redemption of the Object. Divinity, which Analogism had found both in Subject and Object, was perceived as only in the Subject. But this position led to difficulties because there was no way of controlling or setting moral limits to the redemptive activities of the Subject. The temptation was to violate other Subjects in the exercise of his redemptive enterprise, but to do that is to violate the Self, for it exists only by the assertion of other selves.

From this it followed that the Subject did not have a divine authority; it was not the instrument through which Divinity entered the phenomenal world. Stripped of that divine authority, there is left nothing but the naked Subject nakedly exposed to the naked Object. This is the stage I have called Objectism. Its great theme is illusion, the notion that all metaphysics or cognitive models are illusions, that none have transcendental authority. But this situation, as Wagner's *Ring* and Tennyson's *Idylls* demonstrate, suffers, for a different reason, from the deficiency of Analogism. The weakness of that is that it offered nothing but passive acceptance; the weakness of Objectism is that it offered nothing but passive suffering. Value arose only from the endurance of an appalled vision. Cognitive overload is the peculiar experience of the Objectist. It was necessary, therefore, to create a citadel, a strategy of both offense and defense, a means of holding the Self together and of preventing cognitive overload. Yet it had to be a means that was metaphysically indifferent. The next and final stage of 19th-century Romanticism, first appearing in the late 1850's and 1860's, I have called Stylism, rather than the more common term Aestheticism. Style is a universal of human behavior. Yet it is arbitrary and metaphysically indifferent. Thus the creation of a style became the way out of the impasse of Objectism. It gave the individual a goal—looking at the metaphysical emptiness of the Object—but did not commit him to any specific ethical direction or morality. At the same time he could adopt or improvise a metaphysic or a morality for whatever purpose he might have, dropping it when it had done its job. The instrumentalism or pragmatism implicit in Romanticism came to the fore. Both William and Henry James are Stylists.

III

Coming to Hawthorne once again after an interval of twenty years, I was struck by two features. First is the extraordinary quality of Hawthorne at his best. Even *Fanshawe* showed at once that here was a man of astounding literary gifts, and *The Scarlet Letter* is the only novel to which I would ascribe the word "perfect." The second feature was that I encountered no themes with which European Romanticism had not made me familiar. This does not mean that Hawthorne was a mere imitator, or that his version of Romanticism was not unique. But that uniqueness does not make him peculiarly American. The great European Romantics were as different from each other as he was different from them. Each major author—and almost every minor one—discovers, examines, and proposes solutions to the Romantic problems in his own manner.

In his early short stories and sketches Hawthorne was particularly concerned with three Romantic themes—guilt, alienation, and historicism. These three are so intimately intertwined in his work, as in most Romantics, that it is extremely difficult to separate them. In terms of cultural development, Hawthorne, with Byron, is the great exponent of Negative Romanticism, and his efforts to understand the nature of guilt and to devise a strategy to be free from it while preserving its advantages is a central Romantic problem. It can be done only—or at least has been done only—by postulating a Self independent from social role. Once this has been done, the guilt can then be seen as a strategy for achieving the Self; and alienation can be interpreted not as the punishment for guilt but as the opportunity for achieving an independent Self, one which can morally transcend the society and the culture. Guilt and alienation, therefore, are something to be exploited, and one of the most important techniques for that exploitation is historicism. For the Enlightenment moralistic historian, the past was something to be ransacked for good and bad behavioral paradigms, but the Romantic historicist used the past for a double interconnected purpose. On the one hand it was a means for separating oneself from society. As such it has often been criticized as emotionally regressive, as mere nostalgia, and perhaps it would be were it not for the use the Romantic made of that historical separation or alienation. In any institution the individual who knows its history has an instrument for analysis and a means of defense against mindless surrender to its current values. He can be aware of the failure of the institution to fulfill its avowed intentions and its social function. So we find in Hawthorne two kinds of guilt, that of the individual and that of New England society. His first notable exploration of the latter is to be found in "My Kinsman, Major Molineux." The strategy of the alienated by which he relieves his own guilt of alienation by locating guilt in the society is by now a relatively standardized device, but at the time of Hawthorne it was reasonably innovative, particularly in this country. It is a self-justifying strategy in a special sense, for it postulates and confirms the Self in opposition to the Social Role. Romantic historicism, therefore, is never an end in itself but a strategy for placing the current social conditions in an ironic perspective, and Hawthorne's historicism, though it has its particular character, is a standard Romantic variety.

Once the Self has been redeemed from society it can be explored in its own terms, and for this purpose Hawthorne developed his peculiar use of emblematic allegory, which reaches its perfection in *The Scarlet*

Letter. This technique, though Hawthorne's is different from that of European writers, creates analogies between Self and not-self, between personality and the world. It has much in common with E. T. A. Hoffman's work; *The Golden Pot* is thematically and technically Hawthornian. Henceforth Hawthorne's theme is the redemption of the Self through the acceptance and exploitation of what society terms the guilt of the individual but which to the Romantic is society's guilt. The two themes can be seen in their relation to one another if one juxtaposes the virtually contemporaneous "The Maypole of Merry Mount" and "The Minister's Black Veil." Nevertheless, the Romantic Self cannot be established until it has found a relationship with others, and the normal Romantic relationship of this sort is empathy. The Self has no real existence unless it affirms the existence of other selves, and that affirmation is the basis of Romantic morality. The most thoroughgoing exploration of this theme in early Romanticism is to be found in Schopenhauer's *The World as Will and Representation,* published when Hawthorne was fifteen, but not known in the United States for some time. Whether Hawthorne arrived at the perception of empathy by himself or derived it from earlier Romantics is irrelevant. Certainly, it is one of the central themes of *The Scarlet Letter*. Chillingworth is evil because he used, in his comfortless old age, Hester as an object. Thereafter—one of Hawthorne's most subtle points—he is emotionally dependent upon the woman whose Self he has violated. Dimmesdale also has violated both Hester and himself by his failure to acknowledge publicly his guilt and his love. Pearl, however, who has grown up in anti-social innocence and is therefore not human, becomes human and eventually, we are assured, a splendid woman by her sudden experience of empathy for her dying father. Hester, in proper Romantic fashion, accepts her guilt, locates the source of that guilt in society, embroiders her A with great splendor, and becomes a free and self-substantiating Self, transcending the moral limitations of her world. But at the end of the book, in her return to her hut, Hawthorne touches, rather gingerly, the next stage of Romantic development, Transcendentalism, the attempt of the free Romantic Self to re-enter society and to redeem it. That problem was to baffle him for the rest of his life.

In *The House of the Seven Gables*, one of the most magical and exquisitely accomplished works in European fiction, he attempts to deal with the problem with the utmost delicacy. But perhaps that word does him a little too much credit. Perhaps the apparent delicacy is really a gingerliness, as if he were a little afraid to engage too seriously with the theme of social redemption. The House itself and its inhabitants have certain resemblances to Tennyson's "Lady of Shalott" and "Marianna," which are both, particularly the latter, very Hawthorn-esque works, with something of Hawthorne's odd use of emblems. In the "Lady of Shalott" Tennyson is directly engaged with the relation of alienated Romantic to society, of Tower to City. And the House is such a tower. We even have in Holgrove the wandering Transcendentalist artist who redeems the past, the guilt of the social order, and releases the imprisoned, although this was more than the Lady-of-Shalott-as-artist could do. Nevertheless, if this is the theme, those who have been freed from the past and social guilt move not from the tower into the city, but merely into another tower, delightfully modern, to be sure, but also built by Judge Pyncheon on a foundation of social guilt. Are we supposed to be aware of this? I think not. Rather I suspect that Hawthorne got a little more started than he could quite manage.

Hence, perhaps, the element of savagery in *The Blithedale Romance*, in which the theme of social redemption is directly in the foreground, and is thoroughly mauled, and yet regretfully, too. It appears that Hawthorne has so far entered into the second stage of Romanticism—*The House of the Seven Gables* having as one of its central themes decision and action—that the world is no longer seen as having an analogical value but rather as having no value at all. "More and more I feel that we had struck upon what ought to be a truth. Posterity may dig it up, and profit by it." It is typical of many Transcendentalist statements. The artist and the thinker can present models of world redemption, but that redemption can actually take place only in the future. At any rate, the possibility of world-redemption is the only basis for re-entry into society, as Hawthorne indicates in his perhaps too self-consciously amusing remarks about Kossuth.

But another theme begins to appear, a matter which now involved Hawthorne in the gravest difficulties, the theme of American simplification, that notion that was so common among American Romantic

Transcendentalists; not only is world-redemption possible, but America is the predestined place for it to happen. Hawthorne has now emerged sufficiently into the world to encounter directly the peculiar problem of the American artist I have already discussed, the desire for the complexity of high-level culture in an environment turned in the direction of simplification and reductionism. The problem had first appeared faintly in the personality of Holgrave, the photographer, the new man. Further, Hawthorne was by now no longer a provincial. He had been exploring the Romantic themes which had been explored in Europe in the first quarter of the century. Emerging on the European stage, he was, in the 1850's and in Europe, out of phase. The most advanced Romantics had already gone beyond a stage he was just beginning to struggle with. But his further progress was blocked by the confusion between the absurdities of American frontierism, of "*Amerika, du hast es besser,*" and Romantic Transcendental world-redemption. It was not, of course, a confusion from which he alone suffered. On the contrary, he was aware that some baffling snarl was before him. He made four attempts to understand the problem. Three of them proved abortive, and the fourth probably would have failed had he not died. It is not surprising that after his first attempt he should have carried to completion *The Marble Faun.* Here was the theme, or a theme, of *The Scarlet Letter* all over again, in a new setting and in some ways more richly developed, the humanizing power of guilt and empathy. The Faun is a kind of fusion of Hester and Pearl. But at the end of the book he is in prison. There is scarcely a hint of Hester's re-entry into society from above. That is, so long as he did not attempt that Transcendentalist theme, Hawthorne could finish a novel.

His difficulty was that he could not locate his problem. The four abortive efforts, therefore, consist of four permutations of the same factors: the footstep, or the guilt of society; the spider, the guilt of the individual; the elixir of life, the Self; and the inheritance. The first three he could handle easily, but the last was too much for him, for in that emblem was adumbrated two inextricably confused themes, the relation of the United States to England, of America to Europe, and the redemption of society by freeing it from the past. On the one hand he was politically too sophisticated as well as far too alienated to imagine that the self-conception of his proper fellow-citizens as representations of the New Adam was anything but self-inflationary illusion. On the other hand, he was intellectually and culturally too sophisticated, too modern, to be able to enter fully into the Transcendentalist vision, which was already an out-moded stage of Romanticism, at least for the advanced. Moreover, he was apparently unwilling or unable to take the essential step in moving from Transcendentalism to Objectism, the stripping away of divine authority from the Self, the naked exposure of Subject to Object, though, again in a gingerly fashion, he moved in that direction. When Hilda shrinks from Kenyon's daring move that way, is it Hawthorne who shrinks, or is Hawthorne deferring to his public? One of the marks of Transcendentalism is a fantastic extravagance of style, as in *Sartor Resartus* or the music of Liszt. By setting the work in Rome, with its churches and catacombs, and in Tuscany, with its old castles and pagan traditions, Hawthorne achieves the equivalent of stylistic extravagance. I would suggest then that Hawthorne's difficulty with the four efforts to write the same novel lay in the fact that he could neither get to the ultimate weakness of the Transcendentalist position nor move out of it into full abandonment of Soul for Self because in his way was the confusion between Transcendentalism and Americanism. The heart of the problem lay in the frightful paradox of the artist and intellectual in America, which has made it so difficult for the American artist to understand himself as either American or artist, the fact that there seems to be every reason that this country should be a place of magnificent opportunity but is, as one lives in it, so terribly constricting to the kind of man who needs desperately to live at the highest cultural level. Did Hawthorne's illness deprive him of his energy to solve his problem, or did the problem and his failure to solve it make him ill? Or was his real problem his incipient movement into Objectism? Melville's fate was different. He stayed alive, but his later years were grim.

IV

Melville began his writing career at a much earlier cultural stage than Hawthorne did. At first he was controlled by an almost total surrender to the seductiveness of American frontier and crisis values. The theme of "*Amerika, du hast es besser,*" in an increasingly pure Enlightenment mode reaches from *Typee* to a climax in *White-Jacket.* Indeed, these works are classic instances of both American simplification and reductionism and of the spread of Enlightenment ideas in the nineteenth century, just as *Mardi* is a splendid instance of the Enlightenment allegorical fantasy, of which *Candide* is the best example and *Peter Wilkins* the one closest to *Mardi* itself. These works have also another characteristic which indicates that Melville had not yet felt the Romantic problems. They are grab-bag books, like Rabelais, Montaigne, *Don Quixote*, *Tristram Shandy*, and the grab-bag way of organizing a work is still to be found in *Moby-Dick. Pierre*, however, moves in the direction in which Romantic art invariably moves, towards a tightly controlled plan. I would not maintain that one is better than another; it is merely that this change in the way of putting a book together is itself an indication that Melville had entered the world of Romantic consciousness, for the Romantic must control every detail from a single point of view in order to create a symbol of the self-justifying Self. Organizationally, then, *Moby-Dick* is a transitional work, like *Mardi* and *White-Jacket*, in that much could be omitted without damage to the exploration of Melville's central problem, but like *Pierre* in that what appear to be several layers of rewriting move the book in the direction of total thematic control.

This is as it should be, for to my mind *Moby-Dick* is directly concerned with the initial Romantic problems, identity and the immanence of value in the universe, or its transcendence. Who knows what precipitated Melville into the Romantic problems? By 1850 it was too late for a man who had read at all in Romantic literature, as Melville had, to experience the breakdown of the Enlightenment entirely independently and to arrive at Romantic conceptions unaided. Wherever he turned in what was to him modern literature he was bound to encounter them, and he turned, I am convinced, particularly to *The Rime of the Ancient Mariner* and to *Sartor Resartus.* Yet just as it is possible today to read those works without any understanding, it certainly was even more possible in Melville's day. Somehow he had already thought himself to the position where he could use the Romantic tradition.

It is typical of him that he went to the heart of the matter and began at the beginning. He presents in their initial form the great Romantic themes: Ishmael, the wanderer, the loss of goal-direction; the opposition of land and sea, or the sundering of Self from role; the pool of Narcissus, the Romantic rejection of solipsism, whence flows the hard-headed realism and factuality of Romanticism; the enormous amount of exact information, another instance of Romantic factuality; the loss of identity at the masthead, a perfect Romantic assertion that looking up through Nature to Nature's God, the melting together of Subject and Object, is a loss of identity; the survival on the coffin, the Romantic insight that the acceptance of death is the confirmation of the Self; the Romantic rejection of Soul in favor of Self; and finally Ahab, the almost perfect Negative Romantic, who loses his connection with reality by rejecting his role but who has not gained a Self. Probably because he came to Romanticism so late, and, as an American, so freshly, Melville used for Ahab the theme of illusion, which was not used in Europe in the early Romantic stages, except for Schopenhauer, and does not appear generally until Objectism, that is, until the 1840's at at the earliest. Ahab, then, having lost the Enlightenment sense of value immanent in the universe determines either to prove the universe has no meaning or to give the universe meaning by an act, whether that meaning be good or bad. But Ahab is also like a Wordsworth who wants to prove his Analogism, to link beyond breaking the analogies of the Self and the not-Self, and to do this empirically. So, though Ahab has not discovered his Self, it is, we are informed, nevertheless at work within him. Ahab's actions may be condemned but not his motives. But Ahab is also something of an Emersonian Transcendentalist; he is engaged on a hunt which, if successful, would be world-redeeming.

In short, it is as if Melville had absorbed all at once all stages of Romanticism up to his own time, and had presented them in *Moby-Dick* in inextricable confusion. I am inclined to believe that this is why the interpretation of *Moby-Dick* is so difficult and why in all probability it will never be understood with clarity or agreement. It represents Melville's thrashing about in a tangle of culturally emerging ideas the relationships of which he did not understand. The style of *Moby-Dick* is as confused as the analysis of Ahab, and as improvisatory. Nor do I wish to condemn or in the slightest devalue the book on this account. My point has nothing to do with literary quality. It is rather that the various styles are derived from various stages of Romanticism, just as the ideas are; and that much of the later portions of the book are written in a high Transcendentalist style strongly influenced by Carlyle.

Pierre is a work of a wholly different character. It has nothing of the grab-bag plan of *Moby-Dick* and is stylistically consistent. Melville has now more deeply entered into Romantic culture, for the book shows that rigid planning and stylistic over-determination by which the Romantic both symbolized the Self and held it together. Furthermore, it is a style in the high Transcendentalist manner. Today it is not to most people's taste, but then neither is the prose of Carlyle, the poetry of Mrs. Browning, or the music of Liszt. It is the style of Transcendentalist virtuoso extravagance, and different as it is, it derives from the same cultural values as Emerson's *Essays* and Whitman's *Leaves of Grass*. The purest model of this style has always been Paganini, both as man and artist. It is not inappropriate to the theme of *Pierre*. The style of the narrator separates him entirely from the protagonists and their environment. It symbolizes a Self which has transcended that world. It is therefore intended to be of redemptive value to the reader. But I suspect that Melville's relative failure with it as opposed to its success in certain passages in *Moby-Dick* results from the fact that he had already passed the position for which such a style is the proper symbol. Already in the brief appearance of Plinlimmon appears the icy detachment of the Objectist, such as one finds in Baudelaire, which is one of the strategies by which the Objectist naked Self keeps itself intact. This was to be the Melville of the future, the position which he had already sighted, which even in *Moby-Dick* he had dimly glimpsed.

That new vision was to find both its style and its metaphor in *The Encantadas*, the horrible world with the seductive and illusory name, and in *Benito Cereno*, in which the good captain is entirely deceived by the illusions deliberately thrown about him, and in which the truth of the matter is revealed in the form of legal depositions. Illusion is likewise, mildly and amusingly, the theme of *Israel Potter*, and pitilessly of *The Confidence-Man*. The theme of the first half of that work is that we con other people by digging at them until we reach a personality factor which desires illusion; the theme of the second half is that we can do this so well because our principal activity is conning ourselves. Everything cancels out everything. One is reminded of Swinburne's *Atalanta in Calydon,* in which the positions that we should not trust in the world and those that we should, cancel each other out. But *Atalanta* is a work of the Stylist period of Romanticism. The reader as well as the author is protected by a functionless style and a setting remote in time and place. *Pierre, The Encantadas, Benito Cereno,* and *The Confidence-Man* are about America. They are and always have been repugnant to those who have accepted the American simplistic and reductivist myth, which has made Americans so helpless before their major problems, as Melville cruelly points out in *Benito Cereno.*

For these are cruel and bitter works, and they are above all novels about the American problem. Melville, who had now travelled in Europe and shortly was to go again, took the step which Hawthorne could not bring himself to take, the rejection of the American illusion, a step which always costs an American terrible suffering. Few Americans have won their way to the highest level of European culture so rapidly and with such metaphysical grasp, although there were necessarily, because of his timing, confusions on the way. He had now, with *The Confidence-Man,* arrived at a position comparable to Wagner's *Ring* or Tennyson's *Idylls,* or Baudelaire, or the painting of Manet and the first stage of Impressionism. He was now absolutely exposed, with no transcendental authority whatsoever. At the time few Europeans had gone so far. But, as with all Americans, the price for such rapid and isolated development was premature exhaustion, as it had been, one suspects, with Hawthorne, and as it was to be with so many great Americans who were yet to appear.

To the terrible strain of being a foreigner in his own country, was added the almost equal strain of the Objectist position. Melville, therefore, turned to the strategy of Stylism. He did exactly the opposite of what Arnold, his slightly younger contemporary, did at almost the same time. Arnold turned from an Objectist poetry to a Stylist prose. His famous disinterestedness, which he accomplished and celebrated in a delightful prose, is the attitude of the Stylist, detached, observing, not non-commital but rarely recommending action for anyone but himself. Melville, who had been writing prose, turned with remarkable symmetry to poetry, for poetry, far more over-determined phonically and syntactically than nineteenth-century prose, provided the protection, the citadel which Melville needed, just as Swinburne enormously increased poetic over-determinations to create his Stylist manner. It is not surprising, therefore, that Melville should have turned for his first major poetic effort to the Civil War, nor that next he should turn to a consideration of the great religious, metaphysical, and scientific questions of the day. Of the quality of *Clarel* as a poem I wish only to say that I find it something of a scandal that it has never been admitted to its proper place in the canon of major American poems. I found it a delightful work to read, written with great prosodic deftness and imagination, and consistently interesting. To my mind it is Melville's finest achievement after *Moby-Dick*, and it makes considerably more sense. I suppose that what troubles readers, aside from the fact that very few readers, even professional critics and scholars, are well-disciplined in reading long poems, is the discussion of what seem to be long-forgotten issues. I rather suspect, therefore, that it is more interesting to someone who comes to it from a background in English literature of the period, for there is hardly anything, including the diatribes of Ungar against democracy, which is not thoroughly familiar to him. But perhaps to most readers the most baffling thing about it is that none of the issues are resolved. Everything cancels out everything. In this it is remarkably similar to Pater's *Marius the Epicurean*, published nine years later, or *Fifine at the Fair*, by Browning, published four years before, or Morris's Prologue to *The Earthly Paradise*, published eight years earlier. It is even more like Browning's *Parleyings*, published eleven years later, which is an exploration of the various semantic functions of the word "truth," with no conclusions about what truth really is. I rather fancy that the difficulties Melville interpreters have had with *Billy Budd* arise from an insufficient knowledge of *Clarel* and a failure to understand it. The story is an exemplum of the discursive *Clarel*; it shows how, in a critical situation, in which everything should come clear and be focussed, nothing is clear. It is a story deliberately constructed to defy interpretation. It links Melville with Joyce. By revealing the gritty recalcitrance of reality to the desires of man it offers an appeal to the twentieth-century mind. When Melville died, he was at the forward edge of European thought.

JOHN D. SEELYE

5. *The Structure of Encounter*

MELVILLE'S REVIEW OF HAWTHORNE'S *MOSSES*

So intrinsic was the idea of the quest to Melville's creative drive that its use as a motif extends even to his short stories and sketches. It is the pervasiveness of the quest idea, with its attendant themes of initiation and mystery, which is responsible for the parabolic quality of those shorter works, since each of them, in its restricted way, is concerned with the same ontological problems that inspired Melville's greatest fictions, and most of them, similarly, contain some variation on the quest theme.

Because of the modifications Melville imposed upon the quest motif when adapting it to the purposes of short fiction, the conventional roles established in his romance epics are so changed as to be nearly unrecognizable. The quester is not motivated by a fatal enthusiasm for a mistaken absolute, but by simple curiosity. He is not, moreover, a Byronic hero, but is usually a middle-aged professional man—a lawyer, doctor, or salesman—and in the one instance ("Benito Cereno") where the quester is a sea captain, he is a sluggish, self-contented "Jack of the Beach," the antithesis of Captain Ahab. The settings of these stories, also (their "universe"), are restricted to stage-like areas, and the narrative movement is much more circumscribed than that of the romances, a movement enhanced by a quiet, somewhat mannered style. Nevertheless, the questers of the shorter works are all in motion, physically or intellectually—walking, riding, strolling, climbing, or even (in one case) crawling into some secret place of mystery.

One quester sets out to find a crowing cock whose trumpeting has had a powerful effect upon him; another is determined to discover why a harmless scrivener has suddenly stopped reading copy for him; a third is a traveling seedsman who is led, wonder-struck, through a mysterious paper mill hidden in a forbidding New England valley; a fourth is an American in London who penetrates the fastness of the Inner Temple; another American in London visits the annual Guildhall feast; still another American abroad wanders about the decks of a Spanish slave-ship, trying to determine the reasons for the strange misrule he finds all about him. In most of these tales, then, the quester is a "tourist," who, having traveled (or stumbled) into alien territory, encounters something which fascinates or bewilders him. This enthrallment leads to a desire to explore, and exploration results in a superlative discovery.

As in *Moby-Dick*, these stories are structured to focus attention on the object of the quest—the cynosure—which, for its part, serves to gather the disparates of existence. Since each cynosure is a type of omphalos, a mandalic center, Melville often gives it a mystical quality by surrounding it with an atmosphere of enchantment, as with the doubloon in *Moby-Dick*. The cynosure, similarly, is often located in a metaphorical "chamber," a place difficult to enter and which sometimes has a peculiar little doorway reminiscent of the mysterious entrance to Fairyland. In one sketch, "The Apple-Tree Table," this business is accentuated by the discovery, "in a corner of [a] glen-like, old terraced garden [of] a large and curious key, very old and rusty," which fits the "huge, old-fashioned lock" of the door to a long-closed attic. The narrator, having found the key, voices the dominant theme of these stories: "Now, the possession of a key to anything at once provokes a desire to unlock and explore; and this, too, from a mere instinct of gratification, irrespective of any particular benefit to accrue." This pattern of fairytale atmosphere and aroused curiosity appears in Melville's work from *Typee* on. In his short stories, as elsewhere, it enhances the dominant themes of illusion, quest, and the consequent shock of recognition.

The degree to which this pattern dominates Melville's shorter work is best demonstrated by an examination of an essay which, along with his letters and journals, has generally been regarded as an autobiographical document. This essay, Melville's long review of Hawthorne's *Mosses from an Old Manse*, is actually a carefully contrived work of art whose proportion of fact to fiction is comparable to *White-Jacket* and *Redburn* (if not *Pierre*). Although the background of the review is factual (that is, Melville read and was excited about the *Mosses*), its structure adheres closely to the quest pattern, an adherence which extends even to the metaphors and images with which Melville amplified his record of encounter. Moreover, like that other apparent non-fiction, *Typee*, the essay is sufficiently larded with gratuitous inclusions to remove it from the realm of conventional reviews. As always, in order to tell the truth, Melville was inclined to alter facts.

The most obvious evidence of fictional content in the review is the pseudonym with which it is signed: "A Virginian Spending July in Vermont." As Edmund Wilson has observed, Melville "for the purposes of his essay, assumed a fictitious character. He was not a Southerner but a New Yorker." Another fictional addition, dictated by the pastoral atmosphere with which the review is saturated, is the "Virginian's" claim that he was given Hawthorne's book by a pretty country maid named "Cherry." In point of fact, Melville was given the book by his aging Aunt Mary. Finally, Melville had a wider (and deeper) acquaintance with Hawthorne's work (and perhaps with Hawthorne himself) than the "Virginian" admits to. A year previous to the writing of the review, he had borrowed *Twice-Told Tales* from Evert Duyckinck, and mention of Hawthorne and this work appears in *White-Jacket.* There is evidence that Melville had met Hawthorne before he began the review, that his enthusiasm for the book was inspired by his admiration for the man. "I never saw the man," claims the "Virginian," which, along with the other variances from fact, does not make Melville a liar. It does indicate, however, that as in the case of his other *personae*—from "Tommo" in *Typee* to "Ishmael" in *Moby-Dick*—Melville is here framing a device which will allow him to depart from biographical fact whenever the exigencies of metaphor demand it.

The metaphor which dominates the review is the same compound of enchantment and discovery which enhances so many of Melville's quest stories. The *Mosses*, like his other cynosures, puts forth a great power of attraction, reflecting the dark magician hidden within. "A man of a deep and noble nature has seized me in this seclusion," declares the "Virginian," "His wild, witch-voice rings through me." As in "The Piazza," the consequent exploration of this magical "noble nature" unfolds in a wildwood, "a mile from any other dwelling [and] ... surrounded by mountains, old woods, and Indian pools." By repeatedly punning on the word "nature," Melville establishes a metaphorical complicity that will prevail throughout the essay. Thus, the use of natural imagery extends to Hawthorne's name: "Hawthorne" is a mossy tree that drops seeds and sends down roots. There is a good deal going on, moreover, in this particular orchard, as we shall presently see.

The second, and most important metaphorical element is the journey which underlies the movement of the review, and which is given additional significance by a series of exotic, often pastoral figures borrowed from the dominant figure. Although the Virginian has traveled to Vermont, he has only begun his pilgrimage (like the "seedsman" in New England). His literal journey may have come to an end, but with the discovery of the mystical terrain in the *Mosses*, the Virginian sets out on a second voyage: "It is curious," he remarks, "how a man may travel along a country road, and yet miss the grandest or sweetest prospects by reason of an intervening hedge, so like other hedges, as in no way to hint of the wide landscape beyond. So has it been with me concerning this Hawthorne, this most excellent Man of Mosses." Even such a detail as the Virginian's having read Timothy Dwight's *Travels in New England* serves to substantiate this extended conceit.

Once having made the initial discovery of the mystic landscape beyond the "hedge," the Virginian, like Melville's other questers, plunges headlong into the wild, intriguing countryside of the *Mosses*: by reading Hawthorne's tales, by observing certain indirections, he obtains clues whereby he can "enter . . . into the intricate, profound heart where they originated," a heartscape bathed by a "wild moonlight of contemplative humor," yet containing a deep melancholy that "rests like an Indian-sumner, which, though bathing a whole country in one softness, still reveals the distinctive hue of every towering hill and each far-winding vale."

The merging of pastoral imagery and the travel motif opens eventually into a more ambitious metaphor: Hawthorne's is the National

Soul, his "noble nature" is the American wilderness. "The smell of young beeches and hemlocks is upon him; your own broad prairies are in his soul; and if you travel away inland into his deep and noble nature, you will hear the far roar of his Niagara." There is a certain grotesque humor at work here, as in many of Melville's sketches, but the "Virginian" is quite serious: Hawthorne's soul contains mountain peaks that match the Rockies, an inner range that soars "to such a rapt height as to receive the irradiations of the upper skies," and, as well, an intellect so profound that it "drops down into the universe like a plummet." Mountain-like, eagle-like, Hawthorne's soul is also a microcosm, the "hither side" of which, "the other side—like the dark half of the physical sphere—is shrouded in a blackness, ten times black." The Virginian, like Ahab, is fixed and fascinated by this darkness, which "but gives more effect to the ever-moving dawn, that forever advances through it and circumnavigates the world."

The heart of Hawthorne corresponds to the heart of the *Mosses*, where "contraries" (lights and darks) meet and mate. This is the aesthetic apprehension of paradox: light enhances shadow, shadow defines light. Such is the unifying irony of Melville's vision, which here shapes his metaphorical "review" of Hawthorne's book. In the terms of the emergent figure, "you may be witched by his sunlight,—transported by the bright gildings in the skies he builds over you; but there is the blackness of darkness beyond; and even his bright gildings but fringe and play upon the edges of thunder-clouds." Hawthorne, like Melville's other grails (like Moby-Dick), contains a marriage of disparates, or polar opposites, and it is this which gives his work its mystic power. Hawthorne projects himself into the fabric of his book, which becomes the totality of Nature: his soul and art contain the contrasting forces of the universe, and like those forces they are not revealed to those who accept without question the illusory "bright gildings," the Indian Summer that Hawthorne's contemporaries (save one) saw in his style. Like Shakespeare, Hawthorne is an adept at the "great Art of Telling the Truth,—even though it be covertly and by snatches." His truth is reserved for the members of a select party, a brotherhood who have been initiated into his mysteries: "It is, mostly, insinuated to those who may best understand it, and account for it."

Melville, throughout this review, is talking as much about himself as he is about Hawthorne. There is no small irony in the Virginian's declaration that "However great may be the praise I have bestowed upon him, I feel that in so doing I have served and honored myself, than him." But this coupling is no mere borrowing of feathers by an upstart crow; it is part of the fraternal conceit suggested by the initiatory quality of the Virginian's quest and culminated by the idea of "the whole brotherhood" of creation: "For genius, all over the world, stands hand in hand, and one shock of recognition runs the whole circle round." Genius is not the monopoly of one individual, nor can one individual disown his place in the universal fraternity of talent. The National Literary Shiloh, perhaps, "is not, and never will be, individually developed in any one man," nor "would it, indeed, appear so unreasonable to suppose, that this great fulness and overflowing may be, or may be destined to be, shared by a plurality of men of genius." The shock of recognition, clearly, is a mutual, joint-stock affair, and the journey into the soul of Hawthorne is a narcissistic plunge; like Ahab's pursuit of the Whale, "it is the image of the ungraspable phantom of life, and this is the key to it all."

Although the overt theme of this review is transcendental, mingled with elements of patriotic federalism (at times the Virginian sounds like a Fourth-of-July orator), it is dominated by a sexual conceit which might be variously interpreted: "this Hawthorne has dropped germinous seeds into my soul. He expands and deepens down, the more I contemplate him; and further and further, shoots his strong New England roots into the hot soil in my Southern soul." The journey, clearly, is a honeymoon in which North and South meet and mate, comparable to the nuptials of Ishmael and Queequeg, a mirror of the sunlit and shadowy soul of the bridegroom. It is this marriage metaphor, further, which occasions the seductive atmosphere of the initial passages—the fragrant, Keatsian haymow to which the Virginian retires that he may seed his hot, Southern soul. "Stretched on that new mown clover, the hillside breeze blowing over me through the wide barn door, and soothed by the hum of bees in the meadows around, how magically stole over me this Mossy Man." It is down into a soul presumably virgin to the writings of Hawthorne that the seductive warlock of the *Mosses* sends his wild witch seeds and attendant roots.

The virgin emblem and the atmosphere of seduction are a generic part of the metaphor of exploration, discovery, and unification which this essay shares with the majority of Melville's fiction. The marriage between the Virginian and the New Englander is, like the wedding of Ishmael and Queequeg, a figurative mating, and—like the compounding of quest and cynosure—it relates Melville's far from simple review to the rest of his fictional encounters. The progress throughout the essay, from the initial description of the "papered chamber" in which the "review" is being written, to the "chambered paper" of the intricate *Mosses*, and on to the final evocation of universal, Transcendental Genius, is a metaphorical enjambment, a union keyed by the elaborate pseudonym, "A Virginian Spending July in Vermont."

MAURITA WILLETT

6. The Letter A, Gules, and the Black Bubble

IF THE RHYTHMS of *The Scarlet Letter* and *Moby-Dick* could be photographed, the chart for Hawthorne's novel would resemble the steadily quavering movements of deeply agitated ripples on a dark pond; Melville's graph would resemble the Atlantic in a storm, its waves high crested and deep crescendoing, finally subsiding into a level of calm somewhere in the distance.

And the endings of the two novels are beautifully one with the rhythms of the respective narratives: their themes, style, and imagery.

At the end of Hawthorne's romance, the scarlet letter still shines luridly, like a royal, dark jewel against a background of sable, which it serves to accentuate. If it is to be equated with the "sweet moral blossom" Hawthorne hopes to find at the end of his tale of human frailty and sorrow, it is pathetically microscopic against the infinitude of darkness. Though described as an ever-glowing point of light, it does not cast out the shadows.

The ending of *Moby-Dick* is similar in its intense concentration upon a point of light, but its effect is considerably different from that of *The Scarlet Letter*. When the ship has disappeared and Ahab's violent struggle against the demonic white darkness is over, the black button-like object, which is Queequeg's coffin, the center of the black bubble at the heart of the creamy vortex caused by the sinking of the ship, upward bursts and saves Ishmael's life. The image of him lying on his life-buoy coffin, like a babe of the sea, rocked in the cradle of the deep, with sharks and sea hawks circling all around him, produces an effect of wondrous calm more soothing than anything Walt Whitman ever fathered out of mullein and pokeweed, and as different in its effect as anything could be from Hawthorne's burning A.

The Scarlet Letter's formal, stately, impassioned, uneccentric prose is the proper sheath for the romantic, legended tale of the Puritan past. The long introductory Custom House chapter is highly instrumental in establishing the connection between that past and Hawthorne's present. The key to this relationship is the figure of the familiar room as a neutral territory where the actual and the imaginary meet. The story, even more appropriately than *The Marble Faun*, might have been called "Transformation." The ghost of the dead surveyor Pue, in his immortal wig, who seems to hand Hawthorne the yellow parchment containing the manuscript of Hester's story challenging him to bring her to life again, is more real than his contemporaries in the Custom House, whose jollity is compared to the phosphorescence of decaying wood. His own age Hawthorne calls an "opaque substance" in need of an artist's imagination to bring it to a transparency. Eternal truth, that is, the small core of felt truth in the form of suffering and love, outlives those men and women who have experienced it and, when revived by the sympathetic artist, burns with a steady glow, not the flickering of a dying fire such as Hawthorne saw in his contemporary surveyor. Guilt for sin extends beyond the lifetime of the sinner and must be expiated, or at least acknowledged, in order that the ghosts be laid.

The story proper continues this imagery of imbuement, permeation, blending, metamorphosis, even metempsychosis. The frail wild rose mysteriously survives longer than the granite and oak of prison doors. Legend is more real than history as fact because it involves personality and extends the influences of the past by communication instead of mechanical antecedence. The question What is reality? and What is dream? is expressed in passages describing Hester on the scaffold. The phantasmagoric forms of her former life in England seem more real to her than her present humiliation. Pearl, throughout the story, alternates between the unreal and the brilliantly imaged. Reality is distorted and inflated when Hester sees the gigantic A in the breastplate at Governor Bellingham's mansion. And, later, at Dimmesdale's midnight vigil, the A, like Donne's Good Friday cross, covers the whole world. Life is unreal to Hester because she dwells in a morbid world of the intellect, and to the minister because his hypocrisy and self-torture make his whole life seem a dream and a delusion. To him, only the sin is substantial. The bond of guilt between the lovers is more binding than their love. Even in the forest the A is more real to Hester than the fact of the minister's presence or love's renewal. They wander in a gloomy maze of evil. And the final confession of Dimmesdale is described in terms of effect, change, and metamorphosis. The military and religious procession is like a pageant viewed by the non-participators Hester and Pearl, with whom the reader stands watching. The minister's melodious, mysterious voice, which lifts up the crowd with it to some kind of communication transcending words as symbols of logical meaning, his fitful spurts of energy, Pearl's upward gaze to her father, described as like "a floating sea bird on long heaves and swells of the sound of his voice," Hester's feeling of separation in rank from this man she has known so intimately, Chillingworth's "rising out of a nether region to snatch back his victim," the kinesthetic sense in the reader that something great is about to occur, and finally the strange drama of the minister's confession and the uncertainty of the throng as to what actually has happened—all tend to give *The Scarlet Letter* an ambiguity and a flexibility harmonious with Hawthorne's ambivalence regarding his Puritan ancestors. But, more significantly, they suggest continuity between past and present and set down the enduring effects of eternal truth, the truth of "being true," of suffering, of love, of heroic courage in spite of doubt and human weakness. Past and present mingle. Truth endures. It is as though the Salem of Hawthorne's Custom House is the Boston once removed of *The Scarlet Letter.* Ancestors live in portraits and in the confessions and imaginative transformations of their successors. Life and death are not so diverse as one might suppose.

The action of Hawthorne's novel is seen as through a glass. As readers we know by Hester's statue-like posture and the omniscient author's account of her thoughts that she is agitated beyond expression by her exhibition on the scaffold. We are told by the same omniscience that the minister is tortured into insanity by Chillingworth in his demonic revenge. We are even shown the characters in the throes of humiliation, agonized remorse, or confession. We hear them talk to one another. Yet the total effect resembles that of a Greek chorus or a messenger's report. The severity is softened; the quavering surface just reveals, as if through a veil, the turmoil beneath.

But the characters suffer no violent wrenching from their graves. The similarity of the scenes to tableaux, the formality of the symbols, the non-violence and gradualness with which the characters undergo the transformations they surely experience in the course of the seven years covered by the story, the conclusion accounting for the later activities of Pearl, Chillingworth's death, and Hester's return and completion of her life at the scene of her experience, the burial of the lovers in two graves with one stone, contribute to the effect of continuity proper for a historical tale which the author wants to relate to his own time. There is no sudden breaking asunder of time or people, as in *Moby-Dick*.

In *The Scarlet Letter* there is no De Profundis, no Job's cry for help. There is no hope in Dimmesdale and little in Hester that a different answer is possible. If one does not demand, he can hardly expect, a reply from the gods. Thus Hester suffers, endures, stoically accepting what life metes out. Though she chooses, the range of her choice is so narrow that the choice does not seem like choice. Only once, in the forest, is there any external rebellion. And it is as unrealistic as the minister's decision to leave with her. On the scaffold she does not argue with the dying man when he shushes her for daring hope for an eternity with him. After it is all over, though she comes back, she evidently never does receive an answer. And Dimmesdale and Chillingworth are even more passive to fate than Hester is.

Against this background of hopelessness, stoic courage, and fluctuation within a narrow gamut of subdued pessimism, the ending is rhythmically and logically the proper aesthetic conclusion. There ought not to be a sharp differentiation between the letter A and the field sable; for, in a sense, the two, though not identical, are one. They reflect the public, subdued, pessimistic tone of the whole sad tale of Hester Prynne and Arthur Dimmesdale, who never did learn the meaning of their earthly sorrow and love. The pathos of the A against the dark is almost sadder than the unrelieved black would have been. The armorial field with its coat of arms suggests that sin is universal, that the royal A, which is also the devil's mark, cannot be erased, and that the Puritans, who have interpreted it dually as adultery and angel, have passed it on to their children because it is the only legacy they have to transmit.

At the end of *Moby-Dick*, Ishmael, who had been "ordained" by fate to take the place of Ahab's bowsman, "for almost one whole day and night, floated on a soft and dirge-like main" until he was picked up by the *Rachel*, which was still cruising for her lost children.

Though Ishmael's salvation is not a universal answer to all men's prayers, certainly not to Ahab—a Catskill eagle, made for the sunlight, who has lost its way in its swoop into a mountain gorge—it is a partial answer to the question whether there is any answer at all to any man's cry for certainty in this world. The answer seems to be that there is no final certainty of knowledge. And that whatever certainty is possible does not bring happiness to man. Bulkington, who seems to have known more about some things than anyone else in the story, was a far from happy man. But, though there is no certainty of knowledge, human love inactivates the war without and neutralizes the hatred within. Both Ishmael, with the questions of the universe revolving in his head, and Ahab, who would strike through the masks, demand more than a stoic's courage to endure what they cannot understand. Ahab goes down in darkness because, whether of his own volition or the diabolic magic which causes him to believe himself the Fates' lieutenant, crowned with iron and bound to an iron track, he cannot will to choose that "singular insular Tahiti" of human love when it is offered him in the form of Starbuck or Pip, or the Pacific heart of Nature, or the dream of home.

But Ishmael comes to know at last, and retains that knowledge (for good) even while he is telling the story of the White Whale and the heroic but doomed Captain, that Ahab, being human, with the flaw of intellectual pride and his sin of manipulation of others to his own end, had to pay the full price for spurning the brotherhood of man, although too late he learned the nature of his error. Ishmael's respect for Ahab's honesty in refusing to accept a superficial answer from God, man, or nature is clear. And his pity for such precious human potential is even more apparent. Like children, both Ishmael and Ahab demand answers, even when no answers seem possible. For Melville, eternity is always quiet, and the only voice of the Deity is silence. Ahab, unlike Hester and Dimmesdale, refuses to bow his head to fate or the way things are or to die an acquiescent death out of sheer enervation or to lower sad eyes to the world's injustices or to lie down in his gloomy grave. He does not get the answer he seeks but refuses the one he is offered and dies blaspheming the impersonal gods because he himself is capable of love such as they never offer him. On the other hand, Ishmael lies, at the close of the story, at the heart of that magic, murderous circle of sharks and sea hawks, like the baby whale encountered earlier in the story, who lay nursing at his mother's breast in the very midst of the warfare of men and leviathans. But the circular imagery so frequent in *Moby-Dick* suggests that inoculation against the warlike, ravenous, cannibalistic world is only temporary and must be renewed. Ishmael does not say he never went to sea again or never suffered another drizzly November in his soul. But the implication is that, once having known the mystic mixing he experienced on the *Pequod* and the miracle of Queequeg's love, his memory of the intense joy of that reality will serve to protect him against future cynicism. The world will thenceforth be *but* the world and not the wolfish world. The circle suggests that the coil of woe is rewindable and that depression and elevation will repeat themselves again and again. Ishmael is to learn the lesson of Father Mapple that the depth of every woe measures the height of its corresponding delight. At first it would seem that such knowledge ought to carry the most faint-hearted from cycle to cycle eternally. But would it? After the *Pequod*, Ishmael knows what the problem is.

Melville achieves the final effect of the Epilogue through the resolution of the most diverse extremes. *Moby-Dick* abounds in paradoxes and contradictions. Black and white traditionally represent good and evil, but they also cover up their opposites; white, usually associated with softness and beauty and divinity, also means coldness, hardness, and death, both physical and spiritual; the ravenous mouth of the whale exists in the same sphynx-like head that is compared with the Deity; the black coffin of Queequeg is Ishmael's white resurrection.

These vast wave-like motions of *Moby-Dick* accommodate exaggeration, including such far-fetched humor as the cook's sermon to the sharks and Stubb's Queen Mab flights; Ishmael's Yankee eccentricities and wild Platonic theories; epic images of magnitude and depth such as the architectural ones of the caryatids or the Hotel de Cluny built over the Roman baths; or Brobdingnagian ones applied to whales; the most violent metaphysical linkings of unlikes such as Venetian blinds and the whale's mouth, the meadows of brit, the whale skeleton chapel in the Arsacides; wonders such as the whales suspended in the ocean at their love-making, or the squid and the legendary kraken, or the remarkable providence of Ishmael's salvation.

Contrasts exist between images of concentration and relaxation. Ahab is described in terms of intensity, fire, scars, cinders, burnt-out craters, bronze, iron, and close-coiled woe. On the other hand, the expansive, relaxed, biding power of the gods or the white whale with its lovely, leering eyes is expressed in opposite imagery. The demonism of fire, darkness, destruction, is balanced by the alluring softness of beauteous nature and the mysticism of brotherhood. In contrast to the masculine, destructive images are the feminine, conservative ones of the heart of nature: the wedding of the sea and sky, which almost woos Ahab from his quest; the far-off look of Queequeg's dying eyes, rounded like rings of eternity.

The language rises and falls in rhythm with these contrasts. Humor and tragedy alternate, like the white and the black, from the most colloquial to the most eloquent and poetic language of the soliloquies. Instead of the gliding, permeative vocabulary of *The Scarlet Letter*, Melville's diction suggests a breaking through, a leap, a sudden and remarkable metamorphosis rather than a stately transformation. The sermon of Father Mapple, with its leaps and dips, its repetitions of *woe* at least eight times in one paragraph outweighed by the echoing *delight* ten times in the next paragraph; the jeremiads, with their apostrophes and exclamations; alliterations; transposed adverbs modifying their verbs before they get to them; unexpected adjectives, and other marvels of language, prepare the reader for anything from demonic miracles to blessed ones.

The jagged crests and dips of these waves are, however, it is important to observe, eventually resolved into circles and plains. Such levels are possible only because the crests and dips have preceded them, but they themselves are of eternity and contain the woe and the joy in a circle in which the thrust of the one balances that of the other. They are not to be confused with stolidity like Flask's or that of the society from which Ishmael fled for his life, the mob that laughs before the wreck or sees the coin as so many dinners, or fornication as "sin" or mechanism instead of love as a human relationship. The levels of resolved opposites are to be associated with the highest wisdom, the deepest calm, democracy, brotherhood, the master circle which has God as its center and circumference. These levels and circles have something to do with green prairies and eternity. The waves are of this time, this place; the circles are of the forever.

Thus, the ending of *Moby-Dick* is as appropriate aesthetically for Melville's novel as the ending of *The Scarlet Letter* is for Hawthorne's. The letter A, Gules, against the Field Sable is right for the subdued and stoic account of acquiescence by even the most rebellious but least hopeful of the Puritans—Hester. The tone of the novel is sad because inability to act inevitably produces melancholy. And neither Hawthorne nor man can do much about sin. But *Moby-Dick*, in some respects, is an optimistic story in spite of Melville's agreement with Hawthorne that the devil's mark is on all men. Ahab does act; though he is doomed, his resistance is heroic; and melancholy is the last emotion anyone could feel over his final speech. Ishmael, the one elect out of thirty, is saved through no desert of his own (his cry did go up with the rest—he tells us so!). The black bubble has burst upward into light, the appropriate psychological sequel to this tale of great violence and color. The baptism in the creamy pool is at least temporary salvation. Chaos is resolved into quiet. The white magic of love, the pinpoint of light at the center of uncoiling springs of woe, protects temporarily from the concentric circles of sharks and sea hawks; white magic cancels black magic, for a while. The effect is not one of pessimism or the pathos of infinitesimal human good against a background of infinite evil. Ishmael is saved. But when one considers the circumstances, how good is this fact? His life is at the cost of his best friend's death; his "election" can hardly bring perfect joy when his captain, Ahab, who has deserved much more than he to find the answer to existence, has perished still asking "why?" Ishmael's personal salvation is inevitably joyful, for him; but can any universal truth, any usable knowledge, he salvaged from it for other men? And what about the dream he had of men united, their bodies lost in one another's in vats of spermacetti? Just before the end of the voyage, Ishmael had intimations of the infinite regression which may be the paradox of seeming progression, a horror suggested by the figure of the Ixion wheel. Though the ending of *Moby-Dick* is relatively optimistic—from Ishmael's point of view—the germ of the idea that man is eternally losing the ground he seems to be gaining was to breed unresolvable paradoxes for the Melville of *Pierre* and the later writings, which seem to negate whatever consolation there is at the close of *Moby-Dick*. We can only hope that Melville's own earthly cycle ended in his assurance that the gentler truths also exist—that *Billy Budd* belongs, with *Moby-Dick*, to such a phase.

J. DONALD CROWLEY

7. The Artist as Mediator

THE RATIONALE OF HAWTHORNE'S LARGE-SCALE REVISIONS IN HIS COLLECTED TALES AND SKETCHES

FEW OF US would quarrel with Seymour Gross's remark that in the last thirty years our criticism has witnessed a "Hawthorne revival" and that this revival can be said to have begun with Randall Stewart's 1932 edition of the *American Notebooks,* a study which revealed "a more earthly, a more manly, man . . . to replace the traditional conception of [Hawthorne as] a haunted shadow suffering from some psychic wound."[1] In restoring what he then could restore of the original manuscripts, Professor Stewart discovered a more democratic Hawthorne who did not "stand apart from his fellows with grave aloofness,"[2] a non-allegorical Hawthorne who, as his journal illustrated, recorded with "meticulous accuracy and in minute detail his observations of the external world."[3] It was, especially at the time, a more appealing Hawthorne, not hindered by "prudishness and false delicacy" but capable instead of what Stewart called "uncompromising realism."[4] All of these discoveries contradicted the impressions given by Mrs. Hawthorne's 1868 edition of *Passages from the American Note-Books,* which by its omissions and revisions, said Stewart, "seriously misrepresents Hawthorne's character and literary genius."[5] As a result of this analysis, one of the clichés of our criticism is, as Stewart himself has put it, that Mrs. Hawthorne has become the classic example, at least in America, of the genteel Victorian female."[6] In making Hawthorne more attractive to modern literary tastes, Stewart had, consciously or not, attributed to Sophia most of those forms of literary genteelism that previously had sometimes qualified our admiration for Hawthorne's work.

Stewart's views, needless to say, have had a large influence, explicit and implicit, on later criticism. In 1936 Arlin Turner expanded them by suggesting that "certain revisions which Hawthorne made in reprinting after 1842 tales published previously" demonstrate that Mrs. Hawthorne "began to exercise a similar 'purifying' influence on [his] writings soon after their marriage."[7] Among other critics who have sought to dissociate Hawthorne as much as possible from genteel sentimentality is Professor Gross, who in 1955 argued that "The Vision of the Fountain"—a tale he says Hawthorne devotees would prefer to forget—is a parody rather than an example of the incredibly sentimental gift-book tale of the day.[8] Much more recently Professor Fredson Bowers, textual editor of the Centenary Edition of Hawthorne's Works, has restored to *The Blithedale Romance* three manuscript passages Hawthorne himself omitted from the first edition.[9] Bowers' grounds for his emendations are that Hawthorne's revisions had probably been made "in deference to the sensibilities" of his wife and thus, Bowers contends, "could not have been literary."[10] Hence, Stewart's conclusions of several decades ago can be said now to have found their way into the definitive scholarly Hawthorne text. Hence, too, while the modern renaissance of Hawthorne studies has freed him from the old myth of the mysterious psychic wound, it has done so, paradoxically, only at the cost of having saddled him with a wife who could enforce her allegedly disparate literary tastes upon him against his will.

In the light of all this it is puzzling to come upon Stewart's apparently obscure essay in a 1958 Hawthorne issue of the Essex Institute *Historical Collections*. Speaking of his plans for a revised, expanded edition of the *Notebooks*, he analyzes what he calls the "errors" of his 1932 Introduction:

> A good deal can be said for the view that Mrs. Hawthorne was trying not so much to misrepresent her husband, or remake his writing closer to her heart's desire, as to do the kind of revising which Hawthorne himself would have done. Of course, with her sometimes mistaken notions of language, and

Arrowhead when owned by Allan Melville, with the piazza still there. Photograph courtesy of Henry A. Murray.

Hawthorne's red house, later destroyed, but now reconstructed on the Tanglewood Estate. Photograph courtesy of Henry A. Murray.

Print of the Shaker Village at Hancock, near Pittsfield, much as it was when Melville and Hawthorne visited it. Photograph courtesy of Henry A. Murray.

Now braced to support its weakened condition, the famous Round Barn of the Shaker Community still stands where Melville and Hawthorne saw it on their visit to the village. Photograph by Jeanne C. Howes.

Broadhall (now the Pittsfield Country Club) as it was in Melville's time. Photograph courtesy of Henry A. Murray.

Saddleback, or Greylock Mountain, dedicatee of *Pierre*. Photograph courtesy of Henry A. Murray.

"Pierre plunged deep into the woods, and paused not . . . till he came to a remarkable stone, or rather, smoothed mass of rock. . . . It was a breathless thing to see." Photograph courtesy of Henry A. Murray.

". . . a narrow recess of the rocks of Monument Mountain." (J. E. A. Smith, *Taghonic* [1879], p. 318.) "If this isn't the place, it should have been." (Douglas Sackman) From photograph taken September 3, 1966.

> delicacy, she made many revisions which would have been abhorrent to the author. But much of her rewriting was similar —and this point I did not sufficiently stress in the Introduction— to the kind of rewriting which Hawthorne himself had done when he adapted notebook material in his tales and novels.[11]

Plainly, Stewart's statement here represents a retraction of some of his most widely accepted conclusions. It strikes me that this later view comes much closer to the whole truth: although the question of Hawthorne's revisions and their relation to literary genteelism is a complex one, the evidence ultimately weighs heavily on the side of Stewart's later—relatively unknown—suspicions rather than on that of the thesis developed in his 1932 Introduction. Hawthorne's typical revisions in the tales and sketches, like many elsewhere in his works, remind us that what we usually call literary genteelism is in fact an ineradicable part of his art. If the phenomenon was a blight on our nineteenth-century literature, it was also a condition of Hawthorne's best work as well as his worst. We miss the point when, trying to see him as striving for an almost colloquial realism in his notebooks, we attribute whatever excessive elegance and sentimentality there is in his published work solely to either the influence of his audience or the bowdlerizing tendencies of his editors and his wife. We are still wider the mark, I think, when we argue, as Stewart has argued, that "*The Scarlet Letter* would be an even greater book if it had been written in [the] early notebook style" of 1838.[12]

Lacking as we do the manuscripts of *Fanshawe* and all but one of the early tales—that of "The Wedding Knell"[13]—our knowledge of Hawthorne's revisions before 1842 is limited for the most part to those changes he made in the eighteen separately printed tales and sketches he collected in the 1837 *Twice-Told Tales*. Having collated these appearances as well as those in Hawthorne's other two major collections —*Mosses from an Old Manse* (1846) and *The Snow-Image* (1852)—I think it accurate to say that there are really no significant differences in the kinds of changes between those Hawthorne made after 1842 and those he made in 1837 before he even knew Sophia Peabody. Most of his revisions, moreover, fall naturally into those categories by which Stewart describes Mrs. Hawthorne's revisions of the *Note-Books*. In 1837 and later, for example, Hawthorne made changes in the interest of grammatical correctness, some of which, like Mrs. Hawthorne's 1868 changes, are nothing more than the substitution of one construction for another equally correct. While Stewart complains of Sophia's prudishness in changing words such as *dung* to *excrement* and *bellies* and *backsides* to *bodies*, he forgets that *dung*, *bellies*, and *backsides* are terms that do not occur at all in the 1837 tales—or elsewhere—in Hawthorne's published work. Significantly, the far more ethereal word *forms* is much more typical of Hawthorne's own diction even than *bodies*. In the 1837 version of "A Rill from the Town-Pump" Hawthorne deleted the "inelegant" verb *wash* and inserted *cleanse*. It is a revision which, needless to say, makes one wonder just how many of Sophia's 1868 changes Hawthorne would have found "abhorrent." Just as Sophia, worrying about passages relating to sex, substituted *temperament* for *animal desires*, Hawthorne had been wary enough in 1837 to change *sectual* to *sectarian* and *female* to *woman*. And in "The Gentle Boy" he dropped the final subordinate clause in this sentence describing the attack of the Puritan children on the Quaker boy Ilbrahim: "[Ilbrahim's] arms had been raised to guard his head from the storm of blows; but now he dropped them at once, for he was stricken in a tender part."[14] Although the context makes it clear that the boy had been hit in the face and not in the groin, the construction must have involved for Hawthorne a sexual as well as a linguistic awkwardness. Such thinking would not have been peculiar to Hawthorne alone. An overzealous printer, setting type for "The Minister's Black Veil" in the 1852 edition of *Twice-Told Tales*, substituted *busily* for *lustily* in the tale's opening sentence: "The sexton stood in the porch of Milford meeting-house, pulling lustily at the bell-rope."

If in 1868 Sophia excluded from the *Note-Books* what Stewart calls "two rather luxurious descriptions of maternal bosoms,"[15] Hawthorne in 1837 deleted the framework surrounding "Mr. Higginbotham's Catastrophe," one part of which contained what he must have considered "indelicate" material: "I drank a glass of wine and water [the narrator Hawthorne says], and stood at the side-scene, conversing with a young person of doubtful sex. If a gentleman, how could he have performed the singing-girl, the night before, in No Song No Supper? Or if a lady, why did she enact Young Norval, and now wear a green coat and white pantaloons, in the character of Little Pickle? In either case, the dress was pretty, and the wearer bewitching; so that, at the proper moment, I stepped forward, with a gay heart and a bold one."[16] Equally characteristic of Hawthorne's sensitivity to this kind of innocuous issue is his revision of a passage in "The Toll-Gatherer's Day," first published in the *Democratic Review* (October, 1837) and then collected in the expanded 1842 *Twice-Told Tales*. The first version included the following sentiment—Hawthorne's benediction for a newly-married couple: "And when you shall have reached the close of that journey of life, on which you are thus brightly entering, hand grasped in hand, and heart folded to heart, may you lie down together to as sweet and happy a repose, as that queer parting smile on our good old friend's face seems to invoke for you, at the close of this day's journey, its first happy stage!" Living in a world in which "criticks and reviews . . . [were] exercising jurisdiction not only upon the literary but moral blemishes of the authors,"[17] however, Hawthorne in 1842 removed what he thought might be interpreted as prurient: "May your whole life's pilgrimage be as blissful as this first day's journey, and its close be gladdened with even brighter anticipations than those which hallow your bridal night!" To say the revision is nothing more than Sophia's bowdlerization is at best to oversimplify, at worst to distort altogether. Between these two versions is a third, published in the Salem *Gazette* (April 30, 1839), in which Hawthorne merely dropped the reference to the toll-gatherer's "queer" smile: "And when you shall have reached the close of that journey of life, on which you are thus brightly entering, hand grasped in hand, and heart folded to heart, may you lie down to a sweet and happy repose." In the light of this *Gazette* version, which is far more angelic than the first version is earthy, it is possible to see that the final version of 1842 achieves, however innocently, a kind of balance between the less complicated attitudes of the first two passages. In that version the physical and the spiritual are described, albeit not to our tastes, as analogues of one another. The *Gazette* reprint appeared just after Hawthorne's correspondence with Sophia had begun, and the angelic and ethereal quality of the revision there so closely parallels the style of his love-letters at this time that it is difficult not to believe he made this change. The final version, written shortly before his marriage, likewise has its counterpart in the letters he was then writing to Sophia: as Stewart has pointed out, the letters late in the courtship always insist on the relationship between physical and spiritual love.[18] The 1842 version, then, even in its decorousness, can be seen as a kind of celebration of the prospects of his own marriage. More important, all three versions indicate that Hawthorne said in each version what, under the circumstances, it was most natural for him to say.

Another of Mrs. Hawthorne's notebook excisions involves "the record of Hawthorne's fancy, as he watched a lighted window of a boarding house in Boston, that a beautiful damsel might be disrobing in that room"—plainly, from Sophia's point of view, "not a decorous fancy for Hawthorne."[19] Ironically, just such a description does occur in "Sketches from Memory," not only in its 1835 appearance in the *New-England Magazine* but, surprisingly, in the expanded 1854 edition of *Mosses*. Hawthorne is describing the communal sleeping quarters of a canal boat:

> Other, though fainter sounds . . . contributed to my restlessness. My head was close to the crimson-curtain,—the sexual division of the boat,—behind which I continually heard whispers and stealthy footsteps . . . My ear seemed to have the properties of an eye; a visible image pestered my fancy in the darkness; the curtain was withdrawn between me and the western lady, who yet disrobed herself without a blush. Finally all was hushed in that quarter. Still I was more broad awake than through the whole preceding day, and felt a feverish impulse to toss my limbs miles apart and appease the unquietness of mind by that of matter.

Two questions are important here: first, why did Hawthorne, after having been so careful to make other, far more innocent, deletions, fail to remove this passage when he collected the sketch? secondly, what is it about Hawthorne's art that makes his typical large-scale revisions to be deletions? Fortunately, Hawthorne's letters provide a solid answer to the first. The description was included in the 1854 collection because Hawthorne, in Liverpool as consul, did not proofread or otherwise see the sketch before its publication. Having revised the 1846 edition of *Mosses* as printer's copy, he gave his publisher James T. Fields permission to add to the collection "other detached passages" of his very early work in the magazines. His normal caution about such material is evident, however, in his instructions to Fields "to be careful to put in nothing that he does not feel absolutely certain about."[20] The passage is altogether singular in Hawthorne's acknowledged works; he and Fields, obviously, did not feel certain about the same things.

The second question is a much more complicated one, the evidence is more circumstantial, and I can only indicate here the general nature of the answer. So far, our criticism has rested on the assumption that the revisions are deletions because Sophia considered certain passages too inelegant, indelicate, or revealing. That Hawthorne consulted her opinion about general literary matters—even before their marriage—is indisputable; and it was his habit, we know, to read his manuscripts to her. But it is also true that Hawthorne, in his quiet way, was his own man. In 1849, for example, when the formidable Elizabeth Peabody returned the manuscript of "Ethan Brand" because it was unsuitable for her new journal, he did not revise the tale to bring it into conformity with her wishes but, characteristically, sent her "Main Street" instead. And we cannot underestimate the calm conviction behind his Preface to the second edition of *The Scarlet Letter*, where he says, over the commotion caused by "The Custom-House," that he "is constrained . . . to republish [that sketch] without the change of a word." Such statements, seen in the light of the revisions he made as early as 1837, suggest that he could not readily be moved to change or delete words or passages he felt to be important and that what he found in Sophia's opinions was at most a feminine and intensified affirmation of his own tastes.

One of the large facts regarding Hawthorne's revisions that critics have not yet seriously considered is the crucial importance anonymous and pseudonymous publication had for him. The 1837 *Twice-Told Tales* is, of course, the first of his works that carried his name, and, with the exception of "Alice Doane's Appeal," it is the first known instance of Hawthorne's revising his text. This shift—from the privacy of anonymous publication of individual tales in the magazines to the public nature of acknowledged authorship—rather than the intervention of Sophia is what controls Hawthorne's attitude toward such revisions as we have seen.[21] All those tales from which he was later to delete "indelicate" passages Hawthorne had first published anonymously or pseudonymously. Chagrined at having to publish his tales separately—and unremuneratively—in the magazines, Hawthorne simply felt free to say certain things in such printings that he later felt he must omit when he acknowledged the tales in his collections. In acknowledging them there, he was trying to present himself as a literary person. Especially after 1837, Hawthorne had an increasingly acute awareness of his public image; he had likewise an instinctive sense of the difference between private utterance and public statement. In his 1851 Preface to the third edition of *Twice-Told Tales*, he wrote that they are not "the communications of a solitary mind with itself" but are instead "in the style of a man of society" and are "his attempts . . . to open an intercourse with the world."

Hawthorne was, of course, writing at a time when the popular audience was full of a fear of fictionality arising out of Scottish commonsense attitudes. But he was clearly determined, both morally and artistically—as the recurrence of the theme in his works suggests—"to live for his own age" and to address himself to that audience. The strategy he devised in order to do this was in accord with his natural bent as an artist. Although his early projected collections of tales—*Seven Tales of My Native Land*, *Provincial Tales*, and *The Story Teller*—failed, Hawthorne retained what was for him the most important aspect of their framework materials. He came to rely more and more, not on the semi-fictionalized narrator of *The Story Teller*, but on prefaces in which he made increasingly open autobiographical statements. "The Old Manse," "The Custom-House," the 1851 Preface to *Twice-Told Tales*, and the Preface to *The House of the Seven Gables* are, among other things, conscious devices by which he sought to guarantee the reliability of his fiction through the presentation of a reliable narrator—himself. This technique demanded the deletion of various remarks present in anonymously published tales that would have reflected adversely on Hawthorne as the acknowledged narrator. It is illogical not to believe that the strategy was his positive response to, rather than rebellion against, the constrictive tastes of his day. His objections to nudity in contemporary sculpture as well as many of his tales—"The Lily's Quest," "Edward Fane's Rosebud," and "Little Daffydowndilly," to name just a few—show that his tastes were basically in agreement with those standards.

While a number of Hawthorne's attitudes toward art are related to Romantic theories, his revisions manifest his reliance on older, neoclassical principles of rhetoric. For him the transmission of the actual into the imaginative always demanded—as his use of notebook material for his fiction shows—changes toward greater reserve and formality, refinement and delicacy. At Bowdoin he had been heavily influenced by his teacher Samuel Newman, whose *Practical System of Rhetoric* had insisted that "'purity and propriety' were the essential qualities both 'in choice of words' and 'the construction of sentences,' and that the triple basis of taste lay in 'refinement, delicacy, and correctness.'"[22] The rhetorical principle of amplification by which Hawthorne enlarged his journal notes into the stuff of fiction invariably fulfilled the eighteenth-century ideal of decorum. In the first stage of his creative process—jotting down the notes themselves—he was concerned only with the bare outlines of his subject and its relation to him. The notes are, indeed, the "written communications of a solitary mind with itself"; modern criticism has not reminded itself often enough that Hawthorne obviously never intended that those notebooks be published. In what we can call the second stage of his creative process —on the one hand, the conversion of the notes into finished tales and, on the other, the revision of anonymously printed material for acknowledged publication—Hawthorne habitually viewed his work "rhetorically:" he viewed it, that is to say, in relation to his audience, an audience with grave misgivings about fiction, some of them similar to his own. Nearly all of his large-scale revisions indicate his desire to mediate between his art and his audience, to guarantee the value of his fiction by virtue of his own reliability as narrator.

Admiring as we do the openness that allowed, say, F. Scott Fitzgerald to publish *The Crack Up* in *Esquire,* we are perhaps understandably suspicious of a rhetorical strategy of mediation such as Hawthorne's. Hence, I think, our attempt to ascribe his revisions to his wife. We should begin to wrestle with the fact that Hawthorne himself made them. In "The Old Manse" he wrote: "So far as I am a man of really individual attributes I veil my face; nor am I, nor have I ever been, one of those supremely hospitable people who serve up their own hearts, delicately fried, with brain sauce, as a tidbit for their beloved public." It is easy for us to see that, given the standards of his audience, Hawthorne's strategy of mediation—his transformation of a private style into a public style—was almost a necessary one; it is more difficult to exercise our historical imagination and see that it was also, for Hawthorne at least, a deeply personal and honest one.

JOHN H. MC ELROY

8. *The Conventionality of* The Scarlet Letter

BETWEEN 1823 and 1860 no fewer than twenty-eight historical novels with settings in seventeenth-century New England—or Puritan novels as I shall call them—were published in the United States. By 1850, when Hawthorne published *The Scarlet Letter*, eighteen of these Puritan novels had already appeared. It seems unlikely, given Hawthorne's interest in New England history and habit of writing fiction based on New England history, that he would have altogether neglected contemporary novels about the Puritans. A variety of English and Continental influences on his work have been recognized, but his most famous novel has never been examined, so far as I know, in the context of the particular American novelistic tradition to which it belongs.

In terms of that tradition, *The Scarlet Letter* is literally conventional from first to last, for Hawthorne used well-defined conventions of earlier Puritan novels at the beginning and at the end of his novel. In the introductory sketch "The Custom House" he expresses a desire to put himself in his "true position of editor" of Surveyor Pue's manuscript;[1] in the last chapter, a conventionally titled "Conclusion," he presents to the reader that "sweet moral blossom," the moral of the story, which he had told the reader in his opening chapter "may be found along the track [of our narrative]" (48).

Hawthorne introduces the conclusive disposition of the surviving characters of his novel with the authorial declaration: "we have a matter of business to communicate to the reader" (261). Indeed it is a matter of business, stage business. Chillingworth, the twisted villain of the piece, conveniently dies soon after his rival, Dimmesdale, leaving an inexplicably large inheritance to Pearl, who suddenly becomes "the richest heiress of her day, in the New World." When Pearl reached marriageable age, we are told, she found happiness in the same manner as several other young ladies at the end of earlier Puritan novels, that is by marrying a nobleman. (The "armorial seals" on the letters which Hester receives from her grown-up daughter are said to be "unknown to English heraldry" (262). Apparently the reader is supposed to deduce from this that she married among the Continental nobility, perhaps in France or Italy.) The depiction of the "actors" in "the closing scene" of this "drama of guilt and sorrow" is no less conventionally stagy. Dimmesdale declares, "Hester, I am a dying man," and, after the usual last-minute speech of contrition by one who has erred, he utters with his "expiring breath" the standard "final word" of dying sinners—"Farewell!" (254, 257). Pearl—the offspring of "lawless passion" (165)—sheds tears upon her repentant father's cheek. The onlookers weep in "tearful sympathy" (254).

Hawthorne had an eye for the picturesque and performed many a conventional task in his Puritan novel. But in carrying out his duties to his reader, sometimes with a facetious air, he usually managed to make convention serve his own ends. For instance, the conventional account of the discovery of a manuscript becomes a lengthy comment on his feelings about his ancestral home and a variety of other matters close to him.

Actually, in pretending to base his novel on a fortuitously discovered manuscript, Hawthorne had chosen the less used of two conventions. Puritan novels invariably claimed some degree of historical authenticity, and it was standard to claim, as Hawthorne did, "authenticity of the outline" (33), rather than authenticity of all details. But there were two ways for the author of a Puritan novel to establish his general authority. He could strew footnotes along the bottom of his pages to show that he had studied New England history, sometimes even adding an appendix to cite further sources. Or, less commonly, he could proceed as Hawthorne did, by announcing his possession of a historical manuscript which he was simply going to "edit." Hawthorne found his authentic source with relative ease, in the dingy attic of the Salem Custom House. Other authors of Puritan novels had to trek through the mountains of Tennessee, demolish an old chimney, or dig a grave in order to come by theirs. Three authors, however, of whom the gentlemanly James Fenimore Cooper was one, had their manuscripts sent to them through the mails—a much simpler and more genteel procedure. Mindful of the manuscript convention to the end, Hawthorne reminds the reader in the final pages of *The Scarlet Letter* that his novel rests upon "the authority which we have chiefly followed,—a manuscript of old date, drawn up from the verbal testimony" (259).

It should be stressed that the attitude of the author of *The Scarlet Letter* toward the use of conventions was not altogether facetious. The one-sentence moral which Hawthorne selects from among "many morals which press upon us from the poor minister's experience" is obviously a concession to convention. Yet this moral—"Be true! Be true! Be true! Show freely to the world, if not your worst, yet some trait whereby the worst may be inferred!" (260)—is not itself necessarily flippant, for Hawthorne insists throughout *The Scarlet Letter* on Dimmesdale's "falseness." It should also be stressed that Hawthorne at times used very pat conventions without detachment or self-consciousness. An instance of this is his introduction of "the grim and grisly presence of the town-beadle, with sword by his side and his staff of office in his hand." This particular representative of the Puritan law, who emerges from the doorway of the Boston jail "like a black shadow" and clears a path for Hester to the scaffold, was a stock figure in Puritan novels before *The Scarlet Letter*. Without exception he is used as Hawthorne uses him, to represent "the whole dismal severity of the Puritanic code of law" (52). Hawthorne objected to the inquisitorial nature of Puritan law and thought of the Puritans as "a people amongst whom religion and law were almost identical" (50). The eighteen Puritan novels prior to *The Scarlet Letter*, almost without exception, similarly mention and strongly disapprove of theocratic law and its consequences.

Another fundamental convention of Puritan novels between 1823 and 1850 is their two-part structure: the love plot and the historical plot. These two plots were usually of equal importance, and the function of the historical plot was to provide both historicity and adventure. It consisted of either typical episodes from seventeenth-century life or some particular historical episode such as the trial of the witches in Salem, the Pequod uprising, King Philip's War, the overthrow of Governor Andros, or the tribulations of the regicides. Hawthorne's historical plot lacked adventure altogether and, except for the particular historical episode of Governor Winthrop's death, consisted entirely of typical episodes which he, unlike most of his contemporaries, kept subordinate to the much more vital foreground of his love plot. For example, numerous authors of Puritan novels previous to Hawthorne considered and used Indian captivity as a typical seventeenth-century experience. Hawthorne employed this convention not only to account for Chillingworth's crucial absence but also, very unobtrusively, to help establish the historicity of his novel at the outset. The convention frequently provided that the captured lover be rescued or ransomed from the Indians just in time to rejoin his love at some stressful juncture, often just in time to rescue her from some ignominy. Hawthorne used this variation of the convention, but with tremendous irony, since the timing of Chillingworth's return plunges the heroine deeper into ignominy.

The visit to the home of a famous Puritan leader, almost always a governor, was another conventional means of typifying seventeenth-century life. This device had the additional purpose of humanizing the Puritans by depicting their domestic arrangements as more elegant and sumptuous than commonly supposed. Hawthorne's consecutive chapters "The Governor's Hall" and "The Elf-Child and the Minister," like chapters in *A Peep at the Pilgrims*, *Hope Leslie*, *The Regicides*, and *Nix's Mate*, emphasize the attention Puritans gave to creature comforts. The same purpose of humanization is served in the chapters which Hawthorne entitled "The New England Holiday" and "The Procession." Half a dozen novels before *The Scarlet Letter* describe some sort of festive or ceremonial occasion common to seventeenth-century New England—such as a military parade, a Puritan wedding, or the arrival of an English ship—during which, as in Hawthorne's description of the gathering for an Election Sermon, some of the customary "Puritanic gloom" is dissipated (230). In fact, the chief historical implication of Hawthorne's Puritan novel, a novel which centers on the sin of adultery, is that the Puritans were, after all, passionate human beings and not monsters of repression.[2]

Instances of the superstitions of Puritans are also a set feature of the historical novels written about them in Hawthorne's day. This convention, while often serving the purpose of comic relief, was also, of course, another means of establishing historicity. Hawthorne's old crone, Mistress Hibbins, who keeps bobbing up in the story, is typically droll; but, as Hawthorne reminds us several times, Mistress Hibbins was later hanged on account of her quaintness. As in most Puritan novels, Hawthorne's recurring allusions to superstitious beliefs and supernatural episodes serve a serious as well as a comic purpose, the purpose of commenting on Puritan thought. His predecessors in the genre of the Puritan novel shared, without exception, his point of view that the supernaturalism of the seventeenth century was pernicious doctrine. His reason for deploring Dimmesdale's reaction to a meteor resembles commentaries on the Puritan mind in many earlier novels: "In such a case, it could only be the symptom of a highly disordered mental state, when a man, rendered morbidly self-contemplative by long, intense, and secret pain, had extended his egotism over the whole expanse of nature, until the firmament itself should appear no more than a fitting page for his soul's history and fate" (155).

Three Puritan novels published before 1850—*Mercy Disborough, The Salem Belle,* and *Delusion*—display more than ordinary conventional connections with *The Scarlet Letter.* In *Mercy Disborough* the title heroine undergoes trial by water, and as Mercy is thrown into the river to determine whether she is a witch, the Puritan magistrates and ministers unfeelingly watch from the shore; the "multitude" of common Puritan onlookers exhibits "the same unsoftened sternness—the same frigid severity—stamped so deeply upon the Puritan character."[3] The author of *Mercy Disborough,* William Leete Stone, conceived the moral issue in both this scene and a later scene when the heroine is put to the stake, as the conflict between "the stern and unyielding severity of the Puritan church" and "the tender pleadings of compassion" (57). In the execution scene, the same image of a crowd of "unbending Puritans" is given, only this time some of the women in the crowd begin to feel compassion for Mercy. "The sterner visages of the greater number of the Puritan beholders of the coarser sex," however, remain "unmoved during the whole of this heart-stirring scene" of the heroine's impending death by fire (65).

In *The Scarlet Letter* Hester undergoes a comparable ordeal imposed by the stern and unyielding severity of the Puritan church. As in the first crowd scene of *Mercy Disborough*, this Puritan multitude consists of "stern-browed men, and unkindly-visaged women" (54); Hawthorne states that "meager, indeed, and cold was the sympathy that a transgressor might look for, from such bystanders" (50). He emphasizes the relentlessness of the crowd by creating a chorus of harsh females, all "church-members in good repute," to represent the *vox populi* of Puritanism. One member of this Puritan chorus declares that Hester "ought to die. Is there not law for it? Truly there is, both in the Scripture and the statute-book" (51-52). At the end of the novel, however, when Hawthorne repeats the scaffold scene, the Puritan multitude is shown, as it is at the end of Stone's novel, to be capable of compassion. In Hawthorne's climactic scene, the "great heart" of the crowd is "overflowing with tearful sympathy" (254).

The Salem Belle also has interesting correlations to Hawthorne's prominent use of the scaffold scene. The final scene in this novel, like that in *The Scarlet Letter*, describes a confession of guilt made from a scaffold. In this case the "spellbound and awe-struck multitude" which hears Trellison's confession of sin fails to perceive its "solemn truths,"[4] just as "the multitude" in *The Scarlet Letter*, filled with "awe and wonder," listens to Dimmesdale's confession, but fails to perceive the true import of this "false and sin-stained creature of the dust" (257, 259). In *The Salem Belle* Trellison tells the heroine, against whom he has sinned, that, although he is "the chief of sinners," he nonetheless hopes for "pardon from Heaven" (230); similarly, Dimmesdale tells Hester that, despite his deep iniquity, he trusts in God's mercy.

A third novel, *The Witch of New England*, might also have directly affected Hawthorne's use of a Puritan crowd gathered at a place of execution to witness the punishment of a female trangressor. Like *The Salem Belle* and *The Scarlet Letter*, *The Witch of New England* ends with a scaffold scene. The most interesting detail, however, is that the anonymous author of this Puritan novel uses a chorus of women to typify the mood of the crowd. The talk of these three women, as they stand beside the jail door waiting for the witch to be led forth to her death, is just as harsh and vindictive as the talk of the female Puritans in Hawthorne's novel as they await Hester's emergence from jail.

Moreover, the "fierce and unbroken spirit" with which Goody Brown in *The Witch of New England* faces her ordeal[5] is reminiscent of the way Hester confronts her neighbors from the eminence of a scaffold with "a haughty smile, and a glance that would not be abashed" (52-53).

Although Hawthorne was the first to write a Puritan novel about an adulteress, he was by no means the first to write about the plight of a female transgressor in seventeenth-century New England. Nor are Hester's suffering and her isolation from "human sympathy" distinctive. *Mercy Disborough, The Witch of New England, The Salem Belle, Hope Leslie, Rachel Dyer, Ruth Whalley, Naomi, The Puritan and His Daughter*, and *Delusion* are all novels in which the heroine's behavior invokes the harsh retribution of Puritan magistrates and ministers, and deprives her of the community's sympathy. In seven of these nine novels the transgressor is, like Hester, a young, beautiful woman; and in every case except one, she is jailed for her behavior. Furthermore, the suffering of this conventional female transgressor always matures and ennobles her. Explicitly, it makes her feel more sympathetic and charitable toward her fellow human beings. Hester, therefore, in becoming "a Sister of Mercy" (161) follows a conventional pattern.

A number of novels contain the convention on which Chillingworth's characterization is based. A villain consumed by the passion for revenge appears not only in *The Salem Belle*, as previously noted, but also in *Hope Leslie, Mercy Disborough, Ruth Whalley, The Puritan and His Daughter*, and *Naomi*. Like Chillingworth, each of these villains is a jilted lover. Hawthorne's central situation in *The Scarlet Letter* resembles, of course, the conventional triangle of two men in love with the same damsel, but by making Chillingworth a special type of jilted lover, a cuckold, Hawthorne established a much stronger dramatic framework than any of his contemporaries who wrote Puritan novels. A large part of the originality and strength of his design lies in having asked a simple question, "What might have happened in seventeenth-century New England when one of the Saints committed a sin of the flesh?" No novelist before Hawthorne had ever posed such a dramatic question.

Pearl is another character having counterparts in earlier novels. In those nine novels that deal with the witch trials of New England history, it was common literary practice, based on historical fact, to emphasize the role which female children played in accusing the victims; and in all cases this behavior was portrayed as perverse. In similar fashion Pearl perversely points the finger of accusation at Hester and Dimmesdale.

In Mrs. Eliza Buckminster Lee's *Delusion* one even finds a detailed likeness to little Pearl: "The child had always been wayward and strange, and especially indocile to Edith's instructions, although she seemed at times to have a strong affection for her. She was fond of long rambles in the woods, and of basking in the sun along the beach. . . ."[6] Edith, the young woman who adopts Phoebe when the little girl's grandmother dies, has the same attitude toward her charge as Hester has toward Pearl: "Edith felt deeply the responsibility she had assumed in the care and instruction of this child. She knew the tenderness of her own heart, her yielding nature, and feared she should err on the side of too much indulgence" (107).

Phoebe shares Pearl's "wild-flower prettiness" and her perfection as an infant "worthy to have been brought forth in Eden" (*SL*, 90): Mrs. Lee compares her cheeks to "pale blush roses" and her lips to "two crimson rosebuds." The flowery prettiness of little Phoebe's beauty is in striking contrast to an expression of perversity that sometimes comes on her face, as it does also on Pearl's: ". . . with this youthful freshness, which was indeed only the brilliancy of color, there was an expression in her face that marred its beauty. It was coarse and earthly, and the absense of that confiding openness we love to see in children. . . . Edith called the child to her, and kissed her fair cheek; but when she observed [that dark, wayward expression], she turned away with a slight shudder, and something like a sigh." Edith draws Phoebe to her arms, however, and "a few moments of playful caressing brought smiles to the young countenance that nearly chased away the dark expression" (108). Mrs. Lee's authorial comment on Phoebe's perversity makes the possible connection between *Delusion* and *The Scarlet Letter* even more intriguing: "There seems sometimes to be an element of evil in the heart of a child, that would almost persuade us to believe in original sin" (130-131).

On the basis of general and specific likenesses between *The Scarlet*

Letter and earlier works of its type, it seems safe to conclude that Hawthorne knew at least some of the eighteen Puritan novels which preceded his masterpiece, and that they affected his composition of a novel set in seventeenth-century New England. Hawthorne may be said, I think, to have been conscious of working within a particular tradition of American historical novels. Recognizing that he adopted various conventions of this native tradition provides a further means of measuring his talent as a novelist and another way of saying that his was an Olympian but not a Transcendental genius.

ALBERT MC LEAN

9. *Spouter Inn and Whaleman's Chapel*

THE CULTURAL MATRICES OF *MOBY-DICK*

AMONG THE "linked analogies" which permeate the structure of *Moby-Dick*, none is more pervasive or compelling than the analogy of the sea with the mysterious, open, unfathomable dimensions of the universe. Commentators have been aware of the many extensions of this metaphor, and since the publication of W. H. Auden's study of the romantic iconography of the sea,[1] the symbolism of the sea voyage, of islands and islanders, of sailors and sea monsters has been what the whalemen once called "loose fish"—fair game for all. Yet the symbolism of the sea, if one follows the imaginative chain far enough, implies a symbolism of the land, or, to put the problem another way, the tragic and metaphysical outreaching of Melville's seamen-protagonists implies a human condition from which they embark on their courageous and heroic quests. It is this human condition—the contingencies of life in culture as portrayed in the early chapters of *Moby-Dick* to which I would briefly draw your attention.

The connecting link between the sea and the land in the novel is the familiar short chapter which stands at the point of critical transition in the narrative, when the *Pequod*, all preparations for her three-year whaling expedition having been finally completed, sets sail from Nantucket. This chapter, titled "The Lee Shore," eulogizes the pilot, Bulkington, the fearless sailor who had no sooner docked at the close of one long voyage than he signed on for another. For, as Ishmael observes, "the land seemed scorching to his feet." The fate of the intrepid Bulkington, however, is that of "a storm-tossed ship, that miserably drives along the leeward land." The paradox of his character is that while "in the port is safety, comfort, hearthstone, supper, warm blankets, friends, all that's kindest to our mortalities," he must flee the land as the threatened ship must crowd sail in order to avoid the dangerous surf. Like the ship, he must fight "'gainst the very winds that fain would blow her homeward; seeks all the lashed sea's landlessness again; for refuge's sake forlornly rushing into peril; her only friend her bitterest foe!"[2]

This paradox of the shore, the threat implicit in all that is stable, domesticated, and ordered by the will of humanity, the very insidiousness of all "that's kindest to our mortalities," contains Melville's pointed critique of American culture. The experiences of the narrator, Ishmael, as he wanders through New Bedford and Nantucket in these early chapters of the novel are no mere five-finger exercise in preparation for the major opus itself. It is a true prelude, a statement of the significant themes which will dominate the tragic score. At the time of his arrival in New Bedford, Ishmael is a lonely, melancholy and impoverished man seeking temporary relief for his body and soul. New Bedford offers him what American culture, at its lowest common denominator, had to offer the bodies and souls of its uprooted masses —board and lodging for a price at the Spouter Inn and the message of repentance from the pulpit of the Whaleman's Chapel. The Inn and the Chapel, those institutions erected by mankind for protection against all that was inhuman in the universe, become in Ishmael's vision of life, that lee shore which menaces him. Neither the conventional economy by which the body is nourished, clothed and housed, nor the religious practices by which the soul finds its orientation could provide, in his contemporary culture, the ultimate answers which Ishmael required for survival. Each epitomizes in its own way that slavish, treacherous shore which bodes destruction.

To the extent that Ishmael, as narrator of his own tale, depicts culture for the sake of deprecating it he is, of course, the familiar romantic ironist. His protest contains some echoes of Rousseau, Wordsworth, and the early Emerson of the self-reliant years, who had set off against all that they found to be artificial and formalized, that which was natural, personal, and thus expressive. The critique which Melville brings us through his art, however, sounds more deeply into the human condition. As a generation of critics has rightly acknowledged, Melville rejected simple primitivistic notions in his consideration of the role man plays in nature. Quite to the contrary, Ishmael, Ahab and the *Pequod's* crew encounter a vast, inexplicable and alien universe which yields no values by which men can live. The sea, the white whale and the heavens—the total environment beyond the guard rails of the *Pequod* is blurred with strange ambiguities, with enigmas of whiteness and obscurities of blackness. Even among the barbarians who make up much of the crew, there are no simply natural men, contentedly adapting themselves to the dictates of a benevolent nature. The vantage point of all men—the human condition itself—is that of culture, either the tribal and warrior cultures from which the harpooners come, the white Protestant culture of Ishmael and the ship's officers, or the makeshift totalitarianism of the *Pequod* as a microcosmic community. The charge leveled by Ishmael against the economic and religious mores of New Bedford was hardly that invidious comparison of civilization and natural values typical of Emerson and Thoreau.

In its place, and this I believe accounts for the undercurrent of bitterness and world-weariness in the tone adopted by Ishmael during these early chapters, is a devastatingly frank appraisal of the effects upon thinking men of the necessary institutionalization of communal life. It is not the *unnatural* quality of human economic systems and religious modes of belief that threaten man, but rather their inescapable *humanness.* The formalized status quo represented in the novel by New Bedford is the very condition by which Ishmael comes to know himself, both as a human animal requiring security and comfort, and as a soul seeking spiritual prodding and solace. In terms of the analogy of the lee shore, the impending wreck of man as he is tossed in the storms of life is neither a result of his separateness from nature nor his inability to master it. The threat of the lee shore—the threat to Ishmael posed by the Inn and the Chapel—is that he will accept this human identity that they have to offer as final and irrevocable. To accept this identity as the condition of survival, however, is to debase the subjective man—what Bowen has called the "essential self" in Melville's writings[3]—into an object, the product of culture rather than the creature of commitment.

What we learn of Ishmael's experiences in New Bedford gives us few qualms about his denial of his essential self. He is highly tentative and detached, treating his experiences at the Inn in that wry, hudibrastic style which reads so well, and making of his sightseeing in the town and his participation in the service at the Whaleman's Chapel occasions for philosophical revery. Only his espousal of the pagan harpooner, Queequeg—that marriage of souls which has set the noses of our Freudian colleagues twitching with delight—partakes of any degree of personal involvement. And this can be read not only as a comment upon Ishmael's avowed tolerance and latitudinarianism, which strains at but finally swallows tattoo marks and shrunken heads, but also as an ironic comment upon Ishmael's inability to establish any meaningful bond with those of his own kind. Not until Ishmael signs the Articles aboard the *Pequod* does the sense of his apartness dissolve and does he become less the observer and more the participant in human affairs.

Detachment for Ishmael is by no means either indifference or insensitivity. His is a consciousness painfully alive to the condition of man, to his grasp upon mortality and to his attempts to fabricate barriers against this mortality. As a potential suicide—or mock-suicide if that is your reading of the initial chapter of the novel—he is obsessed with images of death, which he manages to find all about him, in the alcohol served at the Spouter Inn, in Queequeg's tomahawk, in the memorials in the Whaleman's Chapel, and in the twin gallows which greet him and Queequeg as they arrive in Nantucket. It is the result of this preoccupation that he is doubly aware of the tools and weapons, the artifacts and architecture, as well as the verbal and ritual forms by which man strives to outlive his mortality.

Ishmael observes and comments upon the clothing that men wear and upon the places where they live, particularly the homes and gardens of the mercantile class of New Bedford, who have been made affluent by the whaling industry. He notes the carving on the bench at the Spouter Inn and watches an old salt busily at work with a jackknife inscribing the image of a ship under full sail upon the surface of the bench. He is impressed with the ornamentation provided by the skrimshander, and by the sundry weapons hung on the interior walls of the Inn—war clubs, spears, whaling lances and harpoons. Some of them, like the harpoon of Nathan Swain, have legends with something of immortality about them. Ishmael records his fascination with Queequeg's harpoon, the razor-sharp blade of which is equally useful for shaving or for lifting steaks off the serving platter at breakfast. He records exactly three of the inscriptions chiseled upon the marble cenotaphs in the Whaleman's Chapel, and takes delight in instructing Queequeg in the meaning of the printed page. He describes with impartial interest the curious design of the bar in the Inn, a representation of the yawning mouth of a whale, and the shaping of the pulpit as a replica of the prow of a ship. He assesses with a practiced eye the quality of handhewn timbers and hand-wrought decorative detail, and the imposition of human demands upon raw lumber in the shapes of benches, tables, pews, beds and a wheelbarrow. Everything about Queequeg interests him, of course, but the two artifacts of the shrunken head and the small black idol, Yojo, receive particular attention. And he is particularly engrossed with two products of a higher craft, two oil paintings to which we shall return in a moment. All of this observation is preparatory to one of the central concerns of the novel as a whole, the detailed and graphic presentation of the art and business of whaling. The interaction of human hands with the material substance of the universe is, for Ishmael, part of that irreducible condition of mankind within which they must meet the terms of their mortality.

The Inn and the Chapel are human constructs, both functional and symbolic in their design. The Spouter Inn, as Ishmael recalls it, "was a queer sort of place—a gable-ended old house, one side palsied as it were, and leaning over sadly. It stood on a sharp, bleak corner, where that tempestuous wind Euroclydon kept up a worse howling than it ever did about poor Paul's tossed craft. Euroclydon, nevertheless, is a mighty pleasant zephyr to any one indoors, with his feet on the hob quietly toasting for bed." Ishmael is driven to reflect upon the story of Lazarus and Dives and the wonder of life that the same wind which makes the outsider shiver and shake induces for the insider the sense of comfort and well-being. Upon entering the public room of the Inn,

Ishmael passes through "a low-arched way—cut through what in old times must have been a great central chimney with fireplaces all round." The partial destruction of this great hearth only symbolizes the loss of domestic and familial security which the dwelling can supply to its residents. It also makes the Spouter Inn an indifferent protector against the cold Atlantic winds, as Ishmael was soon to discover. The public room itself is small and dusky, "with such old wrinkled planks beneath, that you would almost fancy you trod some old craft's cockpits, especially of such a howling night, when this corner-anchored old ark rocked so furiously."[4] As a building which offered for a price physical comfort and society, the Spouter Inn was scarcely better than the ships in which its patrons sailed.

Like the Inn, the Whaleman's Chapel is relatively small. Ishmael notes that there had been little room for an ordinary stairway up to the high old-fashioned pulpit which dominated the sanctuary. Ishmael speculates that the architect, acting upon the suggestion of Father Mapple, had substituted the "perpendicular side ladder, like those used in mounting a ship from a boat at sea." It is this lofty pulpit, made more sacrosanct by the withdrawal of the ladder into it by the minister once he had made his ascent, that characterizes the Chapel. Ishmael asks himself at first if this is not a piece of theatricality. "No, thought I, there must be some sober reason for this thing; furthermore it must symbolize something unseen. Can it be, then, that by that act of physical isolation, he signifies his spiritual withdrawal for the time, from all outwardly worldly ties and connexions?" The very shape of the pulpit, suggestive of "a ship's bluff bows" signifies for Ishmael that "the pulpit leads the world."[5] Simple and modest as the Chapel may be in most respects, its pulpit makes a claim to leadership in human affairs that men find difficult to ignore.

Both of these institutions are presided over by men who represent in their characters and deeds the two matrices of social value that Ishmael encounters. The Spouter Inn takes its narrowness and chill from the personality of its proprietor, Peter Coffin, whose very name gives the death-conscious Ishmael pause for thought. Peter Coffin is an insensitive perpetrator of practical jokes, first planing a bench for use as a bed and then plying Ishmael with cock-and-bull stories about his savage bedfellow. Ishmael holds no grudge against Coffin, maintaining that "a good laugh is a mighty good thing, and rather too scarce a good thing,"[6] but otherwise pays that money-grubbing agent of an acquisitive society no more attention than he deserves. In the Whaleman's Chapel, however, he is duly awed by the idiosyncratic and flamboyant personality of Father Mapple. While the name of Peter Coffin had suggested woodenness of a deadly sort, Father Mapple, like the maple tree from which his name is derived, is a vital being who towers grandly and luxuriantly. His physical isolation in the pulpit, his meditative prayers, the hints of introspection in his sermon, and his broad and sympathetic concern with the woe and delight of the universal human experience point to the richer aspects of the American Protestant experience. Even the rhetorical cadences, the nautical allusions and the scope of his ideas contrast starkly with Coffin's glib and argumentative vernacular.

Such contrasts between the economic and religious spheres of human activity dominate these early chapters. In particular, the two paintings, one in the entry to the Spouter Inn and the other upon the front wall of the Chapel, effect a graphic opposition of values. The first, a "long, limber portentous, black mass of something hovering above three blue dim, perpendicular lines floating in a nameless yeast," puzzles Ishmael upon his initial encounter. "Yet," he asserts, "there was a sort of indefinite, half-attained, unimaginable sublimity about it that fairly froze you to it, till you involuntarily took an oath with yourself to find out what that marvelous painting meant."[7] Against the obscurities of this work are poised the noble simplifications of the one in the Chapel: "a gallant ship beating against a terrible storm off a lee coast of black rocks and snowy breakers." Whereas the painting in the Spouter Inn was murky, dark and indefinite, in the canvas behind the pulpit, "high above the flying scud and dark-rolling clouds, there floated a little isle of sunlight, from which beamed forth an angel's face; and this bright face shed a distinct spot of radiance upon the ship's tossed deck, something like that silver plate now inserted into the Victory's plank where Nelson fell."[8] Quite aside from their artistic function as foreshadowing elements, these paintings stand as visual reifications of two distinct world views—the one that dimly recognizes the struggle of man with his physical environment but discerns little meaning in it other than the anomaly of an exasperated whale about to impale himself on the masts of an already foundering ship. The other view attempts to look beyond the fortuitous events of man's struggle with earthly forces to some superior ray of insight and hope. Both paintings contain ships in states of dire extremity—the significant difference is between the image of a gigantic, menacing whale in one and the humanized, communicative figure in the heavens in the other.

One further point of contrast, already touched upon, is deserving of emphasis. The Inn communicates with its patrons primarily through the lower range of the senses. Ishmael is responsive to heat and cold, the taste of food, and the uncertain and dim glimmering of coals and smoking lanterns. Thus visual experience is limited, as the curious painting in the entry also serves to confirm, and verbal intercourse between the inhabitants remains on a low level. Peter Coffin's discourse is commonplace, the whalemen at breakfast sit around a table in embarrassed silence, Bulkington—the idealized sailor—sits quietly among his roistering shipmates. Only the intimate conversations of Ishmael and Queequeg carry meaning, and they are halting and confused because of the language barrier. In the three chapters concerned with the Whaleman's Chapel, however, the shift toward the use of higher faculties is unmistakable. Ishmael reads the memorial tablets; Father Mapple reads the hymn and the Scripture. The congregation joins in the singing of the hymn. Even the moments of solemn silence in the Chapel which precede the service and conclude it have their effect. And there is the sermon itself, its oratorical values so finely calculated to communicate with the congregation and to move their hearts—all of these are appeals to those ranges of sensory apprehension which are appropriate to psychic, rather than physical needs.

The Inn and the Chapel are the two dominating images of these early chapters, each drawing strength from an appropriate system of social values and each subsuming other images and motifs which are to find later development within the novel. Some readers may prefer to see the dangerous lee shore in the values of the Inn and in that cyclical metabolism by which material man makes his accommodation to his environment. Others may view with even greater suspicion the threat to man's freedom in the values of the Chapel and in that restrictive Protestantism which needles the conscience into confessing its guilt and seeking repentance before an all-powerful God. There is little to preclude either view of these early chapters, but a third alternative does present itself. That is, that neither Inn nor Chapel by itself distorts human experience but that in their rivalry within culture they give the lie to one another. Ishmael appears to accept each as a partial truth—his immediate reactions are seldom overtly critical of either. But as he also makes clear in his willingness to practice and defend Queequeg's religion, and in his perverse willingness to take the 275th lay offered to him by Bildad, barely enough to pay for the clothes that he will wear out on the trip, he finds neither the Inn nor the Chapel adequate answers to his total experience of life. Neither Ishmael nor anyone else in the novel can make a meaningful synthesis of these two diverse kinds of value. Certainly not Bildad, the pious hypocrite, who had, Ishmael tells us, "long since come to the sage and sensible conclusion that a man's religion is one thing, and this practical world quite another;"[9] not Starbuck who insists to his captain's face, "I came here to hunt whales, not my commander's vengeance," but then murmurs to himself, "God keep me!—keep us all!"[10]; not even Ahab whose perversion of a commercial whaling voyage into a personal psychic quest leads not to the truth he seeks but into "the woe that is madness."

What seems clear is that Melville had astutely diagnosed the bisociation which was taking place in mid-nineteenth-century culture. The decline of Puritan polity and dogma, on the one hand, and an accelerating technology, on the other, placed thoughtful men in a position of dire uncertainty. To accept the undeniable reality of the Inn, to accept the fact of man's animal needs, his transient role in a changing culture, and the impending necessity of becoming a specialized worker in a complex economic system, was only sanity and the acknowledgement of one's mere humanity. But was this not also a denial of that other truth, that spiritual condition of man which Father Mapple eloquently presented in his retelling of the story of Jonah and the whale? For Jonah's guilt, which not even flight to Tarshish could alleviate, was that he had denied his mission as God's prophet, and in doing so denied God. Father Mapple draws his two-stranded lesson from the story of Jonah, a lesson which speaks first to the congregation, calling upon them to disobey themselves so that they may obey God, but which speaks secondly and most strenuously to the preacher himself, as articulate pilot of the living God, telling him to "stand forth his own inexorable self" and "to preach the Truth to the face of Falsehood."[11] In other words, mere humility and repentance may suffice for ordinary persons, but for the exceptional man they are not enough: he must embrace a militant evangelism—a prophetic defiance of all within culture which ignores or rejects God.

If the affluent capitalism of the whaling economy had polarized values around material goals, the re-emergence of the prophetic strain in American Protestantism, as signalized by Father Mapple's sermon, polarized the psychic forces which would drive men toward transcendent spiritual goals. The urgency of Father Mapple's appeal to spiritual and moral conviction cannot be overlooked. Ishmael is fascinated by it, as he is by Ahab's demonic version of this same appeal. This prophetic denunciation, initiated by Father Mapple but carried on through the novel by such lesser prophets as Elijah and Gabriel, contributes to a dynamic tension between the values of man as animate being and man as spirit in quest of higher truth. Thus it is that the two fundamental concerns of human beings become, in the radical phases represented by the Inn and the Chapel, antithetical and unreconcilable in their appeal to the hearts and minds of men. Destruction ensues as a matter of course: first the doubt and moral paralysis which affect men of good will such as Ishmael and Starbuck; and then the fanaticism of those who would follow Ahab in replacing all culture with their own wild visions of power and fulfillment.

Seen from this perspective, the message of "The Lee Shore" chapter is simply this: that while the culture values of the Inn or the Chapel are neither right nor wrong in themselves, as participating elements within a society they cannot combine to the satisfaction of a deeply thoughtful man. In the direction of their rivalry lay dissension, anxiety, and cynicism. Only in heroic detachment from their lee shore can the individual find his freedom and seek his truth. In its apotheosis of the calm, silent and stalwart Bulkington, the "Lee Shore" chapter aspires to a more comprehensive view of human existence than is provided by the partial and conflicting values of the land. Ishmael, in his sympathy with the pilot, proclaims that:

> As in landlessness alone resides the highest truth, shoreless, indefinite as God—so, better is it to perish in that howling

infinite, than be ingloriously dashed upon the lee, even if that were safety![12]

F. DE WOLFE MILLER

10. *Another Chapter in the History of the Great White Whale*

THE EIGHTY-ONE "Extracts" which preface Herman Melville's *Moby-Dick* are quite as unusual for fiction as "The Custom House" introduction to Hawthorne's *Scarlet Letter.* Aware of the oddity of such procedure, the author retreats into apologetic humor to excuse the presence of that which, though unusual in fiction, obviously seemed essential to his purpose.

The purpose is basically epical, for Melville by choice and arrangement takes pains to establish the importance of the whale in history. The arrangement is loosely chronological, beginning with the Bible and coming down nearly to date of publication.

Seventy-eight of the eighty-one extracts deal directly with whales. With the exception of a pointed allusion to an all-white whale sighted at Spitzbergen in the seventeenth century, he largely avoided duplicating materials within the book itself. The comments on whales are indeed so random as to reinforce strongly the assumption that their purpose is to document the widespread and long-standing interest in whales. The three extracts which do not deal specifically with whales are concerned with mutiny aboard whaling ships. Some significance lurks in these three exceptions. The plot of *Moby-Dick* contains no mutiny, yet the danger of mutiny, as in the Town-Ho's story, is a heightening factor during all except the early and final chapters of the book. Melville in *Benito Cereno* a few years later realized fully the potential for narrative excitement generated by the threat of violence in the explosive confinement and isolation of a ship's company. He reached the highest point of his narrative skill in the rhythmic suspicions and reassurances of Captain Delano when he was received aboard Cereno's ship.

Insubordination, and its organized manifestation, mutiny, were of course a constant interest to Melville, and it appears now that they may become symbols of his life and thought, for it seems that there will be no end to the argument whether Melville be the grand mutineer.

One of the *Moby-Dick* extracts is from a newspaper account of a mutiny in which colored people of recent savage background take over a whaler. The other two are from two different accounts of a mutiny aboard the whaleman *Globe* in 1824. Two of the survivors, William Lay and C. M. Hussey, jointly published their version of the incident in 1828, *A Narrative of the Mutiny, on Board the Ship Globe . . . and the Journal of a Residence of Two Years on the Mulgrave Islands*. Melville's extract from this gives only the facts that the mutiny was "a horrid transaction" and that the *Globe* was a Nantucket vessel. Melville altered the text in order to inform the reader that the *Globe* was a whaling ship. Twelve years after this account was published, William Comstock, brother to the chief mutineer, brought out another in which the transaction remains "horrid," even as told by a brother. It is with the writings of William Comstock that we are chiefly concerned here. This, his first book, had the elaborate descriptive title, frequent for this type of work: "The/Life/of/Samuel Comstock,/the Terrible Whaleman./Containing an Account of the/Mutiny,/and Massacre of the Officers/of the Ship Globe, of Nantucket;/with His Subsequent Adventures, and His Being/Shot at the Mulgrave Islands./Also,/Lieutenant Percival's Voyage in Search of the Survivors./[Woodcuts]/—/By His Brother, William Comstock./—/Boston:/James Fisher, Publisher,/No. 71 Court Street./Turner & Fisher, New York, and Philadelphia./—/1840."

Another edition of this book, abbreviated to thirty-six pages, was published by Blanchard in Boston, five years later, a year, that is, after Melville returned from the South Seas. It had a brief title, *The Life of Samuel Comstock, the Bloody Mutineer*. Neither edition of this exceptionally rare book has heretofore been identified in Melville scholarship.[2] The most recent annotated edition of *Moby-Dick*, in fact, states that "no source has been found for this extract."[3] Since the passage Melville quotes is identical in each edition, we cannot be sure which he used, for he cites a fact found only in the first—that the author was brother to the mutineer—but has the title of the second.

Though Lay and Hussey's work has long since been listed by Merton Sealts as among the books in Melville's possession—Lemuel Shaw apparently gave him a copy about three months before the *Moby-Dick* manuscript was complete[4]—the story has not been mentioned by any of the numerous critics of Melville's books of the sea. The last half of this book is an account of the experiences Lay and Hussey had while stranded for two years among the savages of the Mulgrave Islands, a part of the Marshall Islands, of which the best known in recent decades have been Kwajalein and Bikini. Lay and Hussey's adventure began eighteen-and-a-half years before that of Melville and Toby Greene. There are numerous similarities with Melville's account of his Polynesian adventure in *Typee*, but the most marked differences are in the fact that Lay and Hussey stayed a much longer time and wrote a much shorter, non-fictional account.

Every devotee of Melville's second most popular book will certainly wish to read this account of whalemen who at the same age as Melville and Toby Greene find themselves precariously safe from the island savages because two families adopt and guard them from repeated threats of the natives, who are at first convulsed with laughter as they crowd in from various communities to see and feel their white skins. The excitement and doubt that attend their escape to a ship lying offshore is quite similar to the rescue Melville describes in *Typee*—and Melville, his adventures over, returns home aboard the same vessel, the *United States*, that had brought William Lay around the Cape. It is not necessary to cite minor similarities, such as the fact that William Lay had his Fayaway too, to show that most readers who like *Typee* will want to read this book also. The ballad that sprung up about Comstock may well have suggested the ballad conclusion to *Billy Budd*. The Lay and Hussey book has been reprinted with a careful introduction by Edouard Stackpole.[5]

Samuel Comstock, the mutineer, was the oldest son in a very respectable Nantucket Quaker family. He was only a few months past twenty when he led the *Globe* mutiny, compromising his younger brother George, a mere lad of fifteen, who was at the helm the night the officers were killed below deck. It is to this younger brother of his that the mutineer made the threat which Melville chose to quote. To keep the boy quiet and force him to steer properly Samuel said, and Melville quoted: " 'If you make the least damn bit of noise,' replied Samuel, 'I will send you to hell!' " (p. 80) The quotation had been copied exactly from Lay and Hussey, and it appeared too without change in the later abbreviated version. Melville's purpose as judged by his choice of quotations from each book is apparently to emphasize the possible dangers aboard a whaling ship, as background for the delicate balance of safety among the crew of the *Pequod.*

William Comstock reports in his Preface that William Lay had told him "several years ago" that neither he nor Hussey had written a word of the book, but that the facts and a fee of $50 had been given to a man of Nantucket who, leagued with people who had suffered by the mutiny, had introduced prejudice and partiality. Lay had offered Comstock $50 more to straighten the matter out for a second edition. This Comstock said he could not do, as he apparently went on a long voyage, probably whaling, himself. Now he writes what purports to be his own account of the mutiny, hoping he says, to extenuate the deeds of his brother. Actually, unless the irrationality of the mutiny or possibly the mutineer's insanity be the extenuation, William Comstock does not remotely succeed in his purpose. He neither omits nor glosses references to his brother's early erratic behavior, and he in no way vilifies the officers who were victims of the mutiny. William Comstock adds to the original story numerous details indicating that Sam Comstock was exceptionally brave and that he fascinated many people, but William never for a moment approves the purposes to which either the bravery or the fascination are applied. Yet they make a better story, and when we note William's frequent sarcasms about his brother's failings we begin to suspect that the true purpose of William Comstock was to obtain grist for a book at the expense of his family. This becomes rather obvious when he concludes his account with the information that after his brother's skull and cutlass were disinterred by officers rescuing Lay and Hussey, these relics were carried back to

New York where they could be viewed in one of the city's museums—one of the museums, no doubt, which inspired P. T. Barnum's great collection of curiosities and monstrosities.

We can be assured that Melville knew both the books about the *Globe* mutiny, for in *Moby-Dick* he speaks of Comstock's as "another version" of the story. The student who wishes to be familiar with what Melville read should then know both the book written by the survivors and the one by the mutineer's brother, for though Comstock uses Lay and Hussey's account of the mutiny item by item and frequently phrase by phrase, he adds many particulars and omits the report of what happened to the two youths while they lived among the savages.

Comstock's first book presumably whetted his ambition to become an author, for three years later he wrote at least part of a work entitled *Whaling in the Pacific*, a chapter of which was published in a Nantucket newspaper August 7, 1843. On that day the weekly *Telegraph* became a daily, and page one, Volume One, Number One was filled with a 2500-word account headed "Whaling in the South Pacific. Encounter with a White Whale. By William Comstock." The title, together with the asterisks introducing the first paragraph and the abrupt beginning, indicates that this is an excerpt from a larger work which of course may not have been completed. No other issues of the early *Daily Telegraph* are known to survive, and the editor of the *Telegraph* made no comment at all when he printed the encounter as the chief offering of his initial number. Nothing is therefore known about the rest of the work.

The excerpt is a fictional account of an unsuccessful attempt to take a white whale, by a captain who overrules the strong objections of his first mate that it would be foolish and dangerous to lower after such a whale.

The discovery of this narrative, then, adds another chapter to the story of the great white whale. Brevity keeps it from being an important account, but it is the only instance before Melville in which the white whale avenges himself upon his hunters and escapes.

The excerpt, which does not include the name of the whale ship, begins as follows:

> * * * * The ship was fanning along with a light breeze, courses

hauled up, whole topsails and top-gallant sails, when a fellow on the forecastle cried out, 'There is a whale close to the ship!'

'Where?' said Mr. Hussey, eagerly. The object was pointed out to the mate, whose countenance fell in a moment. There lay a large whale, within a cable's length of the stern, and Hussey showed no enthusiasm—no ambition—no wish to encounter him. But now, the captain and Swain perceived the object.

'Lines in the boat!' vociferated the captain. 'Captain Coffin,' said the mate, 'did you ever lower away for a white whale?'

'What signifies white or black?' said the intrepid commander. 'Get your boat ready, sir!'

'Captain Coffin,' said Hussey calmly, 'I have followed this business a great many years, and you may depend upon it, that a whale, like the one yonder, makes but little oil, and is very dangerous to go alongside of.'

'We did not come here to talk of danger,' said the captain—'I came for whales, and whales I'll have, when they are to be got.'

'You never saw a white whale before,' said Hussey; 'but I know what they are.'

'That's true,' said the captain thoughtfully, 'I never saw a white whale; but this fellow is as white as chalk—but no matter, get your boat ready, and we'll talk more about it when we come aboard.'

'Some of us,' replied the mate, 'may never come on board again.'

'You are enough to frighten the whole ship's company,' said the captain; 'I hope you are not afraid of a whale.'

'Perhaps so,' answered the mate, with a glowing cheek, 'but you will soon know whether I am afraid of a whale or not.'

With intemperate haste the mate flew to his boat; he called aloud for his crew—tore off the tarpaulin, and seizing the line-tub in his powerful grasp, placed it, without assistance, in the boat.—His boat's crew were assembled, and, for once, Mr. Hussey's boat was manned and lowered before Mr. Swain had got his tub in the boat.

A comic interlude then follows. Ben the ship-keeper, who had breathed sulphur from the very mouth of British cannon, had yet to prove to his shipmates that he was not afraid of a whale. The captain, since the weather is unusually calm, makes Nicodemus Biddy the ship-keeper and allows Ben to take a place in Swain's whaleboat. Biddy's Nantucket wife had been so early and absolutely bored with him that she had managed for fifteen years to get him a new berth immediately upon his losing the last. When Swain had made this adjustment in the crew of his boat, he put off from the ship and

> started upon seeing Hussey already half way to the whale, heaving on the after oar, and vociferating like a madman. Hussey urged on his oarsmen with quick and sudden shouts, and acted, in every instance, so different from his usual manner, that his boat's crew looked at him with undisguised astonishment.—Hussey had always appeared eager when in pursuit of whales; but at this time there was a recklessness and frenzy in his manner, for which they could not account. He ran the boat directly on the whale before he spoke to Coffin,[6] and when he did speak, he cried in a loud and harsh voice,— 'Come aft here, you Coffin—Shiver you! come aft.' But Coffin did not move quick enough for him; and springing into the head, he caught up the boat-steerer, and after throwing him headlong into the stern, seized the irons, and buried them up to the sockets in the body of the whale.

I skip some of the details of the fierce encounter with the whale, during which it pulls Hussey's boat two miles windward. After the other boats overtake them the effort to kill the whale is renewed and Swain and three of his men are injured, the rest of his crew, lost.

> Hussey and the Captain hastened to the relief of the three survivors; but suddenly the whale presented himself, between the boats and the sufferers. 'Pull round the whale!' cried the Captain. But that was not so easily done, for the enraged animal now assailed Mr. Hussey's boat, and ere the danger could be avoided, he seized the frail vessel with his jaws, and ground it to atoms! The principal part of the boat's crew jumped overboard in good time, but Mr. Hussey was observed struggling in the water with blood gushing from his nostrils, eyes, and ears. He turned his face towards the captain—his eyes glared like a meteor—he stretched out his hands, gave

> one loud yell, and sunk forever!—His bowman was never seen after the destruction of the boat, but the remaining four were taken into the Captain's boat unhurt; with Mr. Swain, his bowman, and Starbuck. The ship was about two miles to leeward. A little breeze filled her sails, and the Captain hoped to reach her safely with his desponding men.

The captain's boat now has thirteen survivors in a craft made for six. As they start for the ship, the white whale makes a final attack and destroys the last of the three boats, killing two more men. The eleven survivors group themselves on the floating remains of the boats, two of them assisting the badly injured Mr. Swain. It is then that they realize that the ship is not sailing towards them, and the captain cries out that all will be lost because of Biddy's stupidity.

> 'Not so!' cried Swain's bowman, who was a Nantucket lad by the name of Joseph Barnard—'Not so, sir; I will swim to the ship and show that nincumpoop how to beat to windward.' Barnard left the fragments of boards and oars and struck off towards the ship.
>
> 'Alas!' said the Captain; 'he will never reach the ship; night is coming on, and we shall all perish!'
>
> 'Despair not,' said the suffering Swain, 'Barnard never yet undertook anything without success. He will reach the ship, but he has a long distance to swim, and night will set in before the ship reaches us.'
>
> The ship continued lying aback. The silly wretch who had been entrusted with the ship did not possess sufficient sagacity to put her about, and eleven men would inevitably have perished, but for the intrepidity of JOSEPH BARNARD, who swam two miles, reached the ship in safety, and put her about.
>
> Ere the ship reached the tragical spot, four men had, one by one, become exhausted, and yielded to their fate. The remaining six were taken on board the ship, consisting of Captain Coffin, Mr. Swain, Starbuck, a Cape-Cod-man, and two Nantucket boys.
>
> The Cape-Cod-man died in one hour after his return to the ship. Mr. Swain was taken below in a very exhausted state; and the other survivors were scarcely able to work the ship.

This fictional account is the fourth reference and the third story of the pursuit of the great white whale dating before *Moby-Dick*, not to mention the oral Indian myth of a giant, evil white whale.[7] Emerson's well-known journal entry in 1834 refers to the dangerous Old Tom, which had already been killed. The first fictional account was Jules Lecomte's "Le Cachalot Blanc," discovered by Janez Stanonik in a French magazine of 1837. This story, which the author claims is authentic, relates the killing of a white whale in 1828 by a Nantucket negro who thereby won to wife the beautiful daughter of a Nantucket captain who had lost a relative to the long invincible whale.[8] Two years later—1839—comes the best known story, by J. N. Reynolds in the *Knickerbocker*, and this time the name Mocha Dick appears. The fourth and last known record, Comstock's in 1843, differs from the first two (and from *Moby-Dick*) in the assertion that the white whale was commercially not a good prize.

There is no direct evidence that Melville ever saw Comstock's story, or for that matter, any other published reference to the white whale. Janez Stanonik has demonstrated that there was a substantial body of folklore which Melville had every opportunity to absorb orally, so that he could have written his novel without having seen any published stories of the whale, real or mythical. Comstock's 1843 account is further indication that there was a widespread fable of a dangerous white whale in the South Pacific. It introduces two elements not in the previous stories, which nevertheless appear in *Moby-Dick*—the fact as already mentioned, that the whale survived, and the fact that the first mate opposed the effort to take the whale. In the previous two stories the white whale's reputation merely whetted his pursuers' appetite for glory. Hussey, rebuked by the captain for talking of danger, became like Ahab, unnaturally obsessed in his effort to take the whale and like Ahab died in the ill-advised attempt.

The presence of Comstock's story is of no direct critical significance, but few lovers of America's great novel would wish to be ignorant of its existence. The importance of Comstock's narrative of his brother's experience is more easily recognized.

EDWIN S. SHNEIDMAN

11. The Deaths of Herman Melville

I FEEL THAT I have about as much right to be here in this select company as has a copy of *The Refugee* or *Redburn: or the Schoolmaster of a Morning* to be in a definitive edition of the *Complete Writings*. For my intrusion, you must blame entirely my all-bestowing benefactor, Professor Henry A. Murray, who, in a myriad of wonderful and mysterious ways of which he alone in this world is capable, led me to Melville and, of equal importance in the charting of my own course, to an abiding and appropriate concern with the dark as well as the light compass-headings of the human voyage. And now my travels have brought me to this gam.

A gam is it? I, who should be listening silently in the dark corner of the cabin, have been, with Captain Murray's urgings, emboldened to speak. In this trade-around of tales, the ship that I report from is a curious composite of ill-fated craft: it has torn timbers from the *Pequod*, rotted spars from the *San Dominick*, broken planks from the *Parki*. I speak, of course, about the vessels of death—and would include even fragments from one of Melville's earliest published writings: "The Death Craft." In short, I am the scrivener-mate from the ever-pressing *Thanatopsis*.

Surely, "death" is one of those patently self-evident terms, the definition of which, it is felt, need not detain a thoughtful mind for even a moment. Every adult person knows instinctively what he means by it. The dictionary defines death as the act, or event, or cause, or occasion of dying, or of the end of life, or of cessation. In these terms, by "the death of Herman Melville" one could refer only to a description or a discussion of what occurred to Melville on September 21, 1891—or by legitimate extension, one might choose to include those events and factors which immediately preceded Melville's physical death, or which were causally related to it. But what can one possibly mean by the *deaths* of Herman Melville?

Melville, in *Pierre*, quoting the highest power, provided us with an operational definition of death as "the last scene of the last act of man's play." But perhaps there is more—"the little lower layer." The main issue for this paper is whether or not the *concept* of death need only be dichotomous—granting that the *event* of death involves a distinct irreversible physiological termination and psychological cessation of one's viable existence. Specifically, the question is whether or not it is possible for us to talk about such matters as death equivalents, substitutes for death, and especially partial deaths, such as deaths of aspects of the self.

On the Death Certificate which has been used in the United States and in many European countries for over the last half century, among other entries, there is stated the *cause* of death and *mode* of death. Currently, in the handbook for all those countries that report to the United Nations there are listed some 130 causes of death. These include asphyxiation due to drowning, myocardial infarction, cerebral hemorrhage, etc. More importantly for our present consideration is that in addition to the cause of death, the mode of death is stated. In the current—and in my opinion, grossly inadequate—classification of modes of death, four modes are indicated. They are: natural, accident, suicide, and homicide, the initial letters of which, for your mnemonic convenience, spell N-A-S-H. Each one of us must end up in one of the barren conceptual crypts. It is immediately apparent that the cause of death does not always automatically indicate its mode. For example, one might die of asphyxiation due to drowning in a suicidal, accidental or homicidal mode. But by far the greater inadequacy of this traditional classification of modes of death and in the concept of modes of death itself, lies in the fact that it emphasizes relatively adventitious and often trivial elements in the death of a human being. This is so because it omits entirely the psychological role of the individual in his own demise. The N-A-S-H classification is Cartesian and apsychological in its spirit. For example, it is a relatively unimportant difference to me whether the light fixture above me falls and I am invaded by a lethal chandelier (accidental mode), or someone about me coughs and I am invaded by a lethal virus (natural mode), or someone shoots a gun at me and I am invaded by a lethal bullet (homicidal mode), in light of the fact that I do not wish (intention) any of these to occur. To be blunt about it, my own overriding interest in my own Death Certificate, if by some illogical magic I could ever be permitted to see it, would be almost entirely in the date.

In order to avoid the inadequacies of this conceptual morass, I have proposed, at the Suicide Prevention Center in Los Angeles—an organization which I helped direct for a number of years before I was recently persuaded to move to the Nation's Capitol by the promise of "an opportunity to paint on a broader canvas"—that all human deaths be classified among three types: intentioned, sub-intentioned, and unintentioned. An *intentioned* death is any death in which the decedent plays a direct, conscious role in effecting his own demise. An *unintentioned* death is any death—whatever its determined cause and apparent conventional mode—in which the decedent plays no effective role in effecting his own demise—where death is due entirely to independent physical trauma from without, or to non-psychologically-laden biological failure from within. But most importantly—and what I believe to be characteristic of the vast majority of all deaths—*sub-intentioned* deaths where the decedent plays some, partial, covert, or unconscious role in hastening his own demise. The objective evidences of the presence of these roles lie in such behavioral manifestations as, for example, poor judgment, imprudence, excessive risk-taking, abuse of alcohol, misuse of drugs, neglect of self, self-destructive style of life, disregard of prescribed life-saving medical regimen, and so on, where the individual himself fosters, facilitates, exacerbates, or hastens the process of his dying.

At the Suicide Prevention Center we have participated with the Chief Medical Examiner-Coroner of Los Angeles County in assessing the psychological role of the deceased individual in his own death, especially in puzzling or cryptic deaths or deaths which are equivocal as to mode of death. We do this by careful and selective interview of a number of his surviving relatives and acquaintances.[1] What might be of especial interest to members of the Melville Society is my own attempt to illustrate this procedure, which I have labelled the "Psychological Autopsy," by a detailed analysis of the enigmatic and equivocal death—was it accident or suicide or what?—of Captain Ahab. This analysis appeared in an essay entitled "Orientations toward Death" published in 1963 in the book *The Study of Lives*[2]—a volume written in honor of Dr. Murray by several of his colleagues and former students.

It is important to note that the role of sub-intention is not at all limited to dying behaviors. Indeed, the main point of this presentation is to assert the importance of the role of the individual—his conscious and unconscious needs, conflicts, thrusts—not only in his dying (his death style), but also in his living (his life style), the latter consisting in part of the ways in which individuals (all too rarely nowadays) elevate, ennoble, expand or actualize their lives, or, conversely, the ways in which they (all too often) diminish, narrow, attrit, or truncate aspects of their inner and outer lives, or what we can now explicitly refer to as the partial deaths of their psychic and social selves.

We can be sanguine that Melville would not have, in principle, resisted this concept of sub-intention, certainly not on the grounds of its involving unconscious motivation. Melville was a veritable cerebral-fluid brother of Freud. His *Moby-Dick* and *Pierre*, to name two instances, rest, in no insignificant part, on the concept of sub-intentioned motivations. Consider, from *Moby-Dick*, Melville's explanation of the aboundingly empathic response of Ahab's crew in terms of "their unconscious understandings," which Melville reified as "the subterranean miner that works in us all."

I now further buttress my position with a quotation from our President. Professor Murray, in his paper "Dead to the World: Or the Passions of Herman Melville,"[3] an address which he gave under the auspices of the Suicide Prevention Center in Los Angeles in October, 1963, aware of our studies attempting to relate the permanent cessation of suicide to the temporary interruption of sleep,[4] asked the following questions:

> "Why not some other related condition such as a temporary or permanent cessation of a part of psychic life, the cessation of affect, feeling almost dead, for example; or the cessation

> of an orientation of conscious life, the cessation of social life, dead to the outer world; or the cessation of spiritual life, dead to the inner world, for example. . . It might be well to take account of different degrees or changes of degrees of life, near cessation, as good as dead; or trend toward cessation, dying."

The concept of partial death—death of an aspect of the self—is now the pivotal and critical concept for our consideration. Its manifestations—and again I quote from my authority—are

> ". . . as if the person's primal spring of vitality had dried up, or as if he were empty or hollow at the very core of his being. There is a striking absence of anything but the most perfunctory and superficial social interaction."

This is accompanied by withdrawal from his society, grave social refusal, or even where the fires of feeling are still burning, they burn without glow or warmth, or pleasure-giving purpose. It has to do with repudiation of one's society, of ostracizing people, cutting them dead; it also relates to society's repudiation and ostracism of the person. Thus there are deaths of aspects of the inner self, and deaths of aspects of the outer or social self. Buchanan's failure to find Melville in America—

> "I sought everywhere for this Titan who was still living somewhere in New York, but no one seemed to know anything of the one great writer fit to stand shoulder-to-shoulder with Whitman on that continent. . ."

is a poignant example of Melville's not being totally socially alive, a partial social death which lasted for some "forty torpid years."

This may be the point to supply a brief but clear example of an individual who participated, sub-intentionally, in his own fate—in this case a broken jaw, lucky for him, not lethal. I refer, of course, to Radney, the chief mate of the *Town-Ho*, "the infatuated man [who] sought to run more than half way to meet his doom,"—an excellent example of the moiety of self-participation in the sub-intentioned act.

Parenthetically, we can note that Melville is filled with moieties, partials, and parts, especially of the human body. I quote a few from many:

Moby-Dick: ". . . some deep men . . . are left living on with half a heart and half a lung . . ."

Benito Cereno: ". . . His voice was like that of one with lungs half-gone—hoarsely suppressed, a husky whisper. No wonder that, as in this state he tottered about, his private servant apprehensively followed him."

Mardi: "Now, which was Samoa? The dead arm swinging high as Haman? Or the living trunk below? . . . For myself, I ever regarded Samoa as but a large fragment of a man, not a man complete. And the action at Tenerife over, great Nelson himself—physiologically speaking—was but three quarters of a man."

Melville had an intimate association with the idea of partial death: About it, he might have said: "I am quick to perceive a horror and could still be social with it." It is debatable whether *Moby-Dick* is as much about terminal death as it is about partial death, and especially about suicidal equivalents:

> . . . whenever it is a damp, drizzly November in my soul . . . then I account it high time to get to sea as soon as I can. This is my substitute for pistol and ball. With a philosophical flourish, Cato throws himself upon the sword; I quietly take to the ship.

And again:

> . . . to the death-longing eyes of such men, who still have left in them some interior compunctions against suicide, does the all-contributed and all-receptive ocean alluringly spread forth his whole plain of unimaginable, taking terrors, and wonderful, new-life adventures; and from the hearts of infinite Pacifics, the thousand mermaids sing to them—'Come hither, broken-hearted; here is another life without the guilt of intermediate death; here are wonders supernatural, without dying for them. Come hither! bury thyself in a life which, to your new equally abhorred and abhorring, landed world, is more oblivious than death. Come hither! put up *thy* gravestone, too, within the church-yard, and come hither, till we marry thee'!

Before we turn to Melville's further explications of these qualitative nuances of death in the human spirit (including his own), I shall, as background material, attempt to present some few quantitative evidences of the extent of Melville's interest in the topics of death. I must confess that I present these quantitative data with both serious misgivings and deep trepidations. To reduce the grand scope of Melville's poetic outpourings to chart and figures can only remind one of Whitman's poem, "When I heard the Learn'd Astronomer":

> "When I heard the learn'd astronomer,
> When the proofs, the figures, were ranged in columns
> before me,
> When I was shown the charts and diagrams, to add, divide,
> and measure them,
> When I sitting heard the astronomer where he lectured with
> much applause in the lecture-room,
> How soon unaccountable I became tired and sick,
> Till rising and gliding out I wander'd off by myself,
> In the mystical moist night-air, and from time to time,
> Look'd up in perfect silence at the stars."

Eleven of Melville's books—*Typee, Omoo, Mardi, Redburn, White Jacket, Moby-Dick, Pierre, Israel Potter, The Piazza Tales, Confidence Man,* and *Billy Budd*—were examined, and a notation was made for each of five types of death material.[5] A brief definition and some examples of these five death categories will now be given.

A. Any reference to the death of the chief protagonist, including his wishes about death, his ideation concerning death, threats of death to him (either by himself or by others), or actions which might result in his death.

B. The actual death of specific characters other than the chief protagonists, either in an individual or a group, such as the entire crew of a ship.

C. Any reference to death relating to other than the chief protagonists: Threats of death, actions which might involve the character in destruction, death thoughts, and so on.

D. Death in nature, and references to death in the environment. Examples would be storms, violence, natural destruction. Other examples would include references to the dark, hostile, destructive, death-dealing aspects of nature and of life in general.

E. Discourse on death, including historic references to naval batties where death occurred; philosophic dissertations on death; metaphysical discussions of death.

The result of this study was the tabulation of 1802 references to death. Table I and Figure I reflect these data from among the eleven books. In the Figure, the solid line represents the manner in which Melville distributed the totality of his eighteen hundred thoughts of death *among* these eleven works; the dotted line indicates the relative concentration per page of death talk *within* each of these eleven works. Of what Melville said about death, he seems to have said most of it—about thirty per cent—in *Moby-Dick*, and next most in *The Piazza Tales, Mardi,* and *Pierre*—14, 13 and 12 per cent, respectively. The vast majority—seventy per cent—of Melville's death thoughts is contained in these four books.

The dotted line in Figure I, reflecting the concentration of death talk per page, was computed by comparing the number of death items per book with the number of pages in the Constable Edition of that book, and then reducing those ratios so that their sum was 100 per cent. These data indicate that there was relatively more death talk per page in *The Piazza Tales* and *Billy Budd* than in any other books, and next highest concentration in *Moby-Dick*.

The distribution of the five death categories among the eleven books is indicated in Table II. These data show us that most of the items (36 per cent) were in the "Discourses on Death" category; least (7 per cent) in the "Death in Nature" category. Among the interesting items contained within Table II is the fact that 45 per cent of the death talk in *Pierre* relates to the death of the chief protagonist.

The quality of the references to death varies among the books: *Mardi* is more philosophic, reflecting a fantasied wish for idealization of society; *Moby-Dick* is concerned more with actual death and symbolic substitutes for death as portrayed through the struggle of man with his internal and external environments; *Pierre* obsesses about death in the individual psyche, an introspective accounting of the psychodynamics of death; *The Piazza Tales* also deals with death in the environment, but the environment pitted against man; and in *Billy Budd* the emphasis is on the interplay of death-movements among the chief characters—Billy, Captain Vere, and Claggart.

In brief summary, we found some 1800 death thoughts distributed

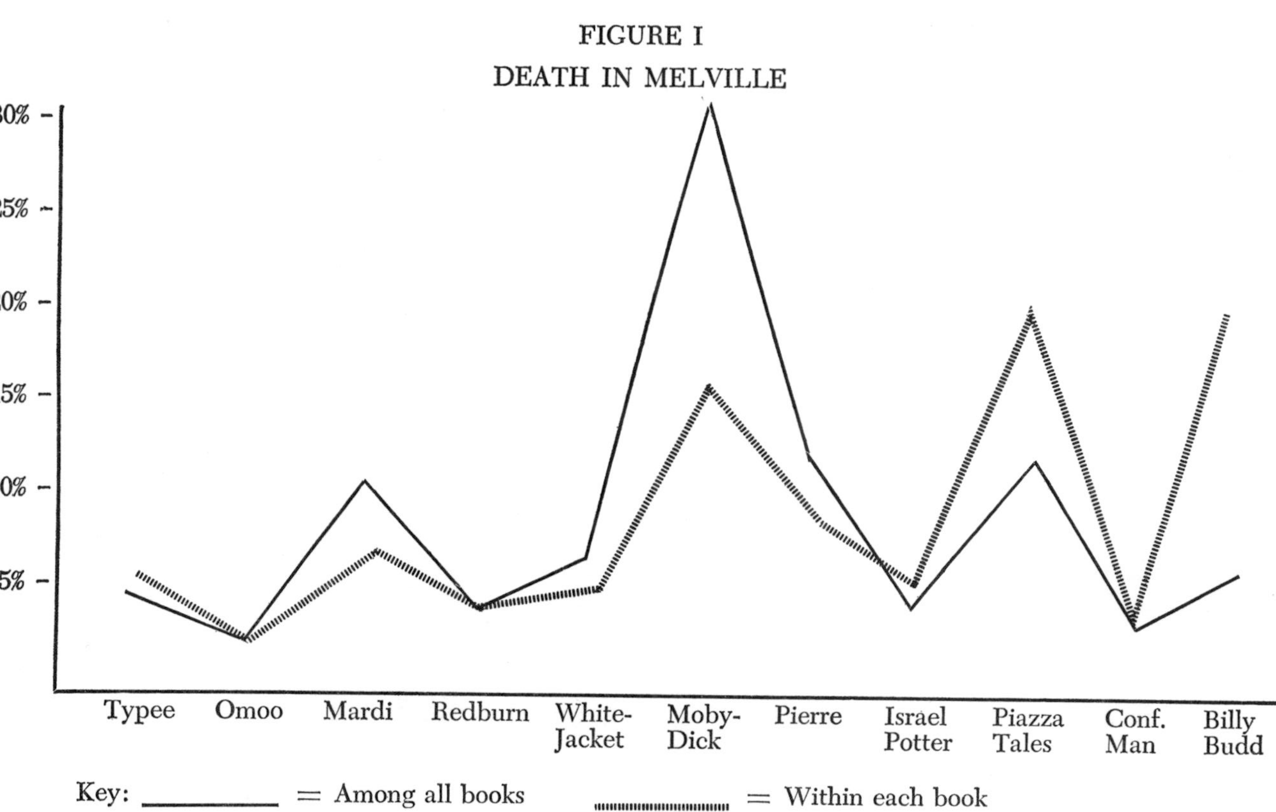
FIGURE I
DEATH IN MELVILLE
30%
25%
20%
15%
10%
5%
Typee
Omoo
Mardi
Redburn
White-Jacket
Moby-Dick
Pierre
Israel Potter
Piazza Tales
Conf. Man
Billy Budd
Key: = Among all books
= Within each book

TABLE II

ANALYSIS OF MELVILLE DEATH ITEMS

	Typee	Omoo	Mardi	Redburn	White Jacket	Moby-Dick	Pierre	Israel Potter	Piazza Tales	Conf. Man	Billy Budd
Number of Items, 1802	92	52	243	89	109	538	218	63	246	49	103
Death Categories:											
A. Any reference to death of chief protagonist, including wishes, ideation, threats, etc.	18%	5%	10%	15%	12%	11%	45%	20%	26%	8%	33%
B. Actual death of specific characters other than chief protagonists.	3%	10%	10%	13%	8%	10%	11%	22%	18%	16%	27%
C. Death in nature; death in the environment.	11%	11%	8%	4%	5%	13%	4%	5%	8%	6%	1%
D. Discourses on death; discussion of death; historic references to death.	28%	31%	51%	37%	43%	26%	34%	32%	29%	57%	33%
E. Any reference to death relating to characters other than chief protagonists: wishes, thoughts, threats.	39%	43%	21%	30%	32%	39%	7%	21%	19%	12%	7%
	100%	100%	100%	100%	100%	100%	100%	100%	100%	100%	100%

TABLE I

DEATH IN MELVILLE

		Among All Books		Within Each Book		
		No. of Items[a]	Per-cent	No. of Pages[b]	% Thoughts per Page	Per-cent[c]
Typee	1846	92	5	340	27	6
Omoo	1847	52	3	375	14	3
Mardi	1849	243	13	769	32	7
Redburn	1849	89	5	403	22	5
White-Jacket	1850	109	6	504	22	5
Moby-Dick	1851	538	30	725	74	16
Pierre	1852	218	12	505	41	9
Israel Potter	1855	63	3	225	28	6
Piazza Tales	1856	246	14	271	91	20
Confidence Man	1857	49	3	336	15	3
Billy Budd	1891	103	6	114	90	20
		1802	100%	4567	456	100%

[a] For five death categories: Cessation of chief protagonist, death of anyone, death in nature, discussion of death, and general cessation.

[b] Constable Edition.

[c] Percentage of thoughts per page divided by 4.5 in order to reduce 456 to 100%.

among some 4500 printed pages of Melville's writing, or about one death thought for every 2½ pages. The most death-laden book is *Moby-Dick*, next *Mardi, Pierre,* and *The Piazza Tales;* the most death-concentrated books are *The Piazza Tales* (which followed *Moby-Dick* by three years) and *Billy Budd* (which followed *Moby-Dick* by almost forty years). Death remained in Melville's mind and flowed from his pen from *Mardi* on, that is, from the time that Melville was only thirty years old.

My saying "only thirty years old" would seem to indicate that some other standards or separate criteria are implied. And so they are. The main notion here is that of an appropriate time of life—an idea based in turn on the concept of stages or phases of life in the total human life cycle. The most famous explication of this notion is in Shakespeare's seven ages of man. In our own time, the psychoanalyst Erik Erikson has written about eight psycho-social stages in the human life cycle; Jung has discussed the two main ages of man; Gerald Heard has described his five ages of man, and Charlotte Buhler has delineated the several main stages in the human course of life, to name a few.

One main point that all these writers imply is that each major period of life is a special time—a time with its own modal special problems, conflicts, crises, ordeals and mysteries. To give one example, adolescence—the teen years—is a time when the main problem is that of separation from the family and the movement into young adulthood, the latter movement carrying with it the problems of how to find and hold love, the role of romantic love and its relationship to sexuality, how to begin a career, and how to establish and support a family.

Building on these concepts, I have elsewhere[6] indicated that psychological crises can occur to a person *within* a period of his life (what I call *intra*-temporal crises); in the interstices *between* periods of his life (*inter*-temporal crises); or, occasionally, there are those crises which occur in individuals who are *out-of-phase* with what ought to be their own period of life (what I call *extra*-temporal crises). This group includes individuals who have "too early" savored experiences "beyond their years," and in this sense, are too old for their age (inappropriately precocious in life-development); and, conversely, it includes individuals who are not "grown up emotionally," who are sheltered not only from experience, but from reflection (retarded in life's ways). These individuals are, in terms of their chronological age, out of tune with the modal psychological issues and conflicts that ought to be occupying their psyches. Experiences that come "too early" (such as at too early an age having to be one's own parents, or having to integrate the impact of sexuality, or having to face annihilation) put one out of phase with one's own years. These individuals may be said to suffer from "information overload" or what might be called "stimulus inundation."

Listen to Melville in early out-of-phase *Redburn*:

> "Talk not of the bitterness of middle-age and after life; a boy can feel all that, and much more, when upon his young soul the mildew has fallen; and the fruit, which with others is only blasted after ripeness, with him is nipped in the first blossom and bud. And never again can such blights be made good; they strike in too deep, and leave such a scar that the air of Paradise might not erase it."

Again, from *Redburn*:

> "I had learned to think much and bitterly before my time; all my young mounting dreams of glory had left me; and at that early age, I was unambitious as a man of sixty. . . Cold, bitter, cold as December, and bleak as its blasts, seemed the world then to me; there is no misanthrope like a boy disappointed; and such was I, with the warm soul of me flogged out by adversity."

Mostly, when Melville was producing these refractory images of his own inner life, his deeper concerns were about his own obsessing intoxication with the enigmatic and unanswerable issues that are more grim even than those of misery and death, namely, eternal and total cessation, naughtment, and annihilation.

And even more and still worse: Had Melville been able to postpone his invested concern with these depressing topics until a more proper time in his own life, he might have been a more measured and sanguine soul, but precocious psyche that he was, he encountered these core issues out of phase with his own life, too early, in his twenties and thirties, and then they could only be for him unconquerable phantoms and monsters, leviathans and krackens.

To answer a soul's need to deal with the issue of one's own annihilation before he is thirty-five is to tackle God's world in off-season, at hurricane time, and then one is faced only with the tortured choice of what nature of wreck will ensue—utter, partial, immobilizing, fatal—but not, alas, with the happier alternatives between wreck or safety, between escape or deep spiritual success, between destructive or positive affective transactions.

On the occasion of Dr. Murray's address in Los Angeles, he stated: "It occurred to me that a roughly analogous study might be made of the . . . cycle of affective transactions in the works of certain Romantic authors—authors whose credo encourages them to give vent in apt and telling words, to emotions of all sorts. I need not tell you the name of my first choice among eligible authors."

I have taken what I consider to be a reasonable calculated risk and assumed that it could have been no other than Melville that he had in mind. If this were so, what can we now say about Melville's credo?

Melville's credo was to say Yes; Yes to his own sense of right; Yes to his fealties to the depths of his own thought and inner experience; but like any other brave man who feels overcome by vastly superior forces, never to say Yes to the commands of others or of fate or of nature to surrender. Melville had several mottoes, for example: *Ego non baptizo te in nomine patris*—you know the rest—but his credo seems to have been this: *better to be drowned as a daring fool than be hanged as an uncommitted or timid coward.* And this, as we shall see, was just a partial reflection of his great, self-ennobling, courage-building, autonomous sense of pride. He voices this credo over and over. But first, concerning his sense of autonomy:

Moby-Dick: "I'd strike the sun if it insulted me."

"I, myself, am a savage, owing no allegiance but to the King of Cannibals; and ready any moment to rebel against them."

". . . the queenly personality lives in me and feels her royal rights. . ."

"Here I am proud as Greek God. . ."

And in a letter to Hawthorne, April 16, 1851:

> "The man who, like Russia or the British Empire, declares himself a sovereign nature (in himself) amid the powers of

> heaven, hell, and earth. He may perish, but so long as he exists, he insists upon treating with all Powers upon an equal basis."

And now, to the core and substance of Melville's credo:

> *Moby-Dick*, about Bulkington: "Better it is to perish in that howling infinite than to be ingloriously dashed upon the lee, even if that were safety."
>
> "Oh man! Admire and model thyself after the whale. Do thou too remain warm among ice. Do thou, too, live in this world without being of it. . . . Retain, O man! in all seasons a temperature of thine own."
>
> *Pierre*: "For now am I hate-shod! On these I will skate to my acquittal! No longer do I hold terms with aught. World's bread of life, and world's breath of honour, both are snatched from me; but I defy all world's bread and breath. Here I step out before the drawn-up worlds in widest space and challenge one and all of them to battle."
>
> *Jimmy Rose*: "I still must meditate upon his strange example, whereof the marvel is, how after that gay, dashing, nobleman's career, he could be content to crawl through life, and peep about among the marbles and mahoganies for contumelious tea and toast, where once like a very Warwick he had feasted the huzzaing world with Burgundy and venison."

And from his letters:

> *June 1, 1851*: *To Hawthorne*: "All Fame is patronage. Let me be infamous: there is no patronage in *that*. . ."
>
> "To the dogs with the head! I had rather be a fool with a heart, than Jupiter Olympus with his head. . ."
>
> *March 3, 1849*: *To Duyckinck*: ". . . then had I rather be a fool than a wise man.—I love all men who *dive*. Any fish can swim near the surface, but it takes a great whale to go down stairs five miles or more; & if he don't attain the bottom, why, all the lead in Galena can't fashion the plumet that will. . ."

Along with his many other ambiguities, Melville, with his great zest for life, was a death-intoxicated man. His concerns with thoughts related to death and diminution appear through his works as a *leitmotif,* subliminally haunting the reader with their baleful expressions of grandeur and woe. Nor are we surprised to find these thoughts in the man who asked so urgently about life's purposes and life's moralities.

What made this issue laden with even more than ordinary anguish was that, for Melville, death meant more than physical demise or even more—if one can imagine it—than psychological cessation; it meant complete, that is, eternal, annihilation. More than do or die; it was exult or never-have-been. The essence of his credo, from Melville's third book, *Mardi*—and one of my own favorite Melville passages—written when he was 29, reads as follows:

> "Oh, reader, list! I've chartless voyaged. With compass and the lead, we had not found those Mardian Isles. Those who boldly launch, cast off all cables; and turning from the common breeze, that's fair for all, with their own breath, fill their own sails. Hug the shore, naught new is seen; and 'Land ho!' at last was sung, when a new world was sought.
>
> "That voyager steered his bark through seas, untracked before; ploughed his own path mid jeers; though with a heart that oft was heavy with the thought that he might only be too bold, and grope where land was none.
>
> "So I.
>
> "And though essaying but a sportive sail, I was driven from my course, by a blast resistless; and ill-provided, young, and bowed to the brunt of things before my prime, still fly before the gale;—hard have I striven to keep stout heart.
>
> "And if it harder be, than e'er before, to find new climes, when now our seas have oft been circled by ten thousand prows—much more the glory!
>
> "But this new world here sought, is stranger far than his, who stretched his vans from Palos. It is the world of mind; wherein the wanderer may gaze round, with more of wonder than Balboa's band roving through the golden Aztec glades.
>
> "But fiery yearnings their own phantom-future make, and deem it present. So, if after all those fearful, fainting trances,

> the verdict be, the golden haven was not gained;—yet, in bold quest thereof, better to sink in boundless deeps, than float on vulgar shoals; and give me, ye gods, an utter wreck, if wreck I do."

In any complete recitation of Melville's unusual combination of gifts, pressures, heritage, and inner thrusts, the role of his private sense of warranted and unwarranted overweening pride must be given the great emphasis it obviously merits. At the outset, we can, following Nietzsche, distinguish pride from vanity—where the former comes mostly from inner feelings and the latter from outside re-enforcement and feedback, as in the case, for example, of poets. With Melville, it is pride, not vanity, which we mean.

It would appear that Melville's inner sense of pride stemmed largely from two main sources: Pride in his family and lineage; but mostly the pride that came from his recognition of his own active, first-rate, self-contained inner life, dealing creatively—and with a sure sense of its own extraordinary capacity—with core cultural and cosmic psychic issues. Melville not only had a self-sustained sense of being of somewhat noble birth, but he also had the feeling of being a more than somewhat gifted man.

His pride in his family is clearly indicated in his books—in *Moby-Dick*, he writes: "It touches one's sense of honor, particularly if you come of an old established family in the land, the Van Rensselaers, or Randolphs, or Hardicanutes."—and explicitly stated in his letters, as, for example, his letter to his mother (May 5, 1870), and to his cousin (August 27, 1876).

As for his pride in himself, as early as 1839, when he was 19, Melville wrote in his *Fragments from a Writing Desk* about his own "mind endowed with rare powers"; all through his letters he writes either with the exaggerated modesty of a proud man or the proper self-respect of a proud man. For example, he writes to his father-in-law: "I hope the perusal of this little narrative of mine will offer you some entertainment." He describes himself in his letters as "conceited," "garrulous," filled with "selfishness" and "egotism." He was hungry to read the reviews and notices of his own works. He wrote to his brother to send him "every notice of any kind" and to John Murray to send him all the reviews of his books. He had an enormous appetite for recognition and fame. Melville was obviously deeply wounded by the critics of *Mardi* and of *Moby-Dick*. After the *New York Literary World*'s review of *Moby-Dick*, he cancelled his subscription to that journal.

Now, if one believes in the power of the self-fulfilling prophecy, the role of pride can be a salutary one. It enhances one's self-confidence and increases effectiveness, but the negative side of this coin is that it also makes one vulnerable. It is like an Achilles heel in an Olympic athlete.

The enemy of pride is criticism, rejection, verbal abuse. I need not take the time in this presentation to recite the criticisms which were levelled at the heart of Melville. The public, represented by the critics, liked his tobacco and wood-chopping works but railed and hooted when he wanted to say the things most meaningful to him. We all know his letter to Hawthorne in 1851:

> "What I feel most moved to write, that is banned,—it will not pay. Yet, altogether, write the other way I cannot."

And, from *The Confidence Man*, the tale of Charlemont, a story of aristocratic pride—and its concomitant fear of dependency and vulnerability, the key lines of which are:

> "When both glasses were filled, Charlemont took his, and lifting it, added lowly: 'If ever, in days to come, you shall see ruin at hand, and, thinking you understand mankind, shall tremble for your pride; and, partly through love for the one and fear for the other, shall resolve to be beforehand with the world, and save it from a sin by prospectively taking that sin to yourself, then will you do as one I now dream of once did, and like him will you suffer. . . ."

In a situation where one has been verbally abused and behaviorally constrained, one can generally react in one of two global ways. He can protest and advance his best efforts and products, but if he takes this course he demonstrates how deeply he cares and how grievously he has been hurt. This tack will make him more vulnerable, more pitiable, and often subject to more abuse. It is a course which runs directly counter to the instincts of a proud man. The other course is to be disdainful, ignoring one's critics as though they did not exist, as though they were dead, reducing them to the unimportant position of impotence by robbing them of their power to influence and especially of their power to hurt. But this maneuver, by its very nature, tragically can be executed only at the price of one's own total or partial self-ostracism and thus at the expense of the death of part of one's social and hence psychological self.

In Stedman's Introduction to the 1892 editon of *Typee*, we read a contemporary illustration of Melville's social death:

> "Mr. Melville would have been more than mortal if he had been indifferent to his loss of popularity. Yet he seemed contented to preserve an entirely independent attitude, and to trust to the verdict of the future. The smallest amount of activity would have kept him before the public; but his reserve would not permit this. That he had faith in the eventual reinstatement of his reputation cannot be doubted . . . Our author's tendency to philosophical discussion is strikingly set forth in a letter from Dr. Titus Munson Coan to the latter's mother, written while a student at Williams College . . . The letter reads in part:
>
> ". . . 'when I left him he was in full tide of discourse on all things sacred and profane. But he seems to put away the objective side of his life, and to shut himself up in this cold north as a cloistered thinker.' "

One human experience not inconsistent with pride is hate or hostile affect. Hostility can take many forms, including verbal criticism, verbal retaliation, physical abuse, and in its most extreme form, complete disregard of the other person—especially conscious disregard. There is great reciprocity in interpersonal or intergroup hostility and, as we know, great danger of escalation of this type of reciprocity. Some hostility is retaliatory, but much of hostility is anticipatory—to get one's blows in first. Melville had more than his fair share of hate—conscious and unconscious: against his parents—his mother and father for separate reasons—against society, and against Christendom—all the forces that he saw as wanting him to surrender and to acquiesce. Granted that his global hate was long repressed by his fear of retaliation; but who can gainsay his attacks on Christianity in *Omoo*, and on Western society in *Typee*?

We see this combination of pride, fear and hate in Ahab's address to the Candles:

> "Oh! thou clear spirit of clear fire, whom on these seas I as a Persian once did worship, till in the sacramental act so burned by thee, that to this hour I bear the scar; I now know thee, thou clear spirit, and I know now that thy right worship is defiance. To neither love nor reverence wilt thou be kind; and e'en for hate thou canst but kill; and all are killed. No fearless fool now fronts thee. I own thy speechless, placeless power; but to the last gasp of my earthquake life will dispute its unconditional, unintegral mastery in me. In the midst of the personified impersonal, a personality stands here. Though but a point at best; whencesoe'er I came; wheresoe'er I go; yet while I earthly live, the queenly personality lives in me, and feels her royal rights, But war is pain, and hate is woe. Come in thy lowest form of love, and I will kneel and kiss thee; but at thy highest, come as mere supernal power; and though thou launchest navies of full-freighted worlds, there's that in here that still remains indifferent. Oh, thou clear spirit, of thy fire thou madest me, and like a true child of fire, I breathe it back to thee."

Nor need we look too far, nor inappropriately exercise our imagination to divine Melville's attitudes about duplicity and criticism, and especially about critics.

> *White-Jacket*: "How were these officers to *gain glory*? How but by a distinguished slaughtering of their fellowmen? How were they to be promoted? How but over the buried heads of killed comrades and messmates?"

> *White-Jacket*: "Do you straighten yourself to think that you have committed a murder, when a chance falling stone has often done the same? Is it a proud thing to topple down six feet perpendicular of immortal manhood, though that loft living tower needed perhaps thirty good growing summers to bring it to maturity? Poor savage! And you account it so glorious, do you, to mutilate and destroy what God himself was more than a quarter of a century in building?"

> *Moby-Dick*: "There's a most doleful and most mocking funeral!

> The sea-vultures all in pious mourning, the air-sharks all punctiliously in black or speckled. In life but few of them would have helped the whale, I ween, if peradventure he had needed it; but upon the banquet of his funeral they most piously do pounce. Oh, horrible vulturism of earth! from which not the mightiest whale is free."

> *Encantadas*: "If some books are deemed most baneful and their sale forbid, how, then, with *deadlier* facts, not dreams of doting men? Those whom books will hurt will not be proof against events. Events, not books, should be forbid."

And from his letters:

> *April 23, 1848*: *To Lemuel Shaw*: "I see that *Mardi h*as been cut into by the London Atheneum and also burnt by the common hangman in the Boston Post."

> "There is nothing in it, cried the dunce, when he threw down the 47th problem of the 1st book of Euclid—there's nothing in it. —This with the posed critic."

> *Dec. 13, 1850*: *To Evert Duyckinck*: ". . . I don't know but a book in a man's brain is better off than a book bound in calf—at any rate it is safer from criticism."

> *Jan. 18, 1886: To John W. Henry Canoll*: "For what can one do with the Press? Retaliate? Should it ever publish the rejoinder, they can."

Perhaps his penultimate comment, from *Moby-Dick*, about the revengers in life:

> "Sharks . . . like hungry dogs 'round a table where red meat is being carved."

And for pure, undiluted heartbreaking hate, no other passage in our literature is so concentrated as this one from *Moby Dick*:

> "All that most maddens and torments; all that stirs up the lees of things; all truth with malice in it; all that cracks the sinews and cakes the brain; all the subtle demonisms of life and thought; all evil, to crazy Ahab, were visibly personified, and made practically assailable in Moby Dick. He piled upon

> the whale's white hump the sum of all the general rage and hate felt by his whole race from Adam down; and then, as if his chest had been a mortar, he burst his hot heart's shell upon it."

For some, the often highly exciting and sometimes superb narrative novels—*Typee*, *Omoo*, *Redburn*, *White Jacket*, *Israel Potter*—remain primarily as valued interstices between Melville's more profound identity-seeking and death-focused labors, those works that sprang out of his deeper shaping and crushing concerns, cemented as they were to both his self and his *post-self*.

The self or ego relates to the core of one's active functioning, his cognitive and emotional masterings and maneuvers in the present life; the post-self, on the other hand, refers to the ways in which one might live on, survive, or have some measure of impact or influence after the event of his own physical death—for example, through one's children (in whom Melville did not before their deaths seem to have that deep an investment, and in whom, after the premature deaths of his sons, he could not have any hope), or through one's published works, in a selected few of which Melville most was deeply invested.

Here are some samples of Melville's thoughts concerning the concept that I have labelled the post-self:

> *Redburn*: "Peace to Lord Nelson where he sleeps in his mouldering mast! but rather would I be urned in the trunk of some green tree, and even in death have the vital sap circulating round me, giving of my dead body to the living foliage that shaded my peaceful tomb."
>
> ". . . how much better would such stirring monuments be full of life and commotion, than hermit obelisks of Luxor, and idle towers of stone; which, useless to the world in themselves, vainly hope to eternalize a name, by having it carved, solitary and alone, in their granite. Such monuments are cenotaphs indeed; founded far away from the true body of the fame of the hero; who, if he be truly a hero, must still be linked with the living interests of his race; for the true fame is something free, easy, social, and companionable. They are but tombstones that commemorate his death, but celebrate not his life. . ."
>
> *Moby-Dick*: "It may seem strange that of all men sailors should

be tinkering at their last wills and testaments. . . After the ceremony was concluded upon the present occasion, I felt all the easier; a stone was rolled away from my heart. Besides, all the days I should now live would be as good as the days that Lazarus lived after his resurrection; a supplementary clean gain of so many months or weeks as the case might be. I survived myself. . ."

". . . I now leave my cetological System standing thus unfinished, even as the great Cathedral of Cologne was left, with the cranes still standing upon the top of the uncompleted tower. For small erections may be finished by their first architects; grand ones, true ones, ever leave the copestone to posterity. . ."

". . . immortality is but ubiquity in time. . ."

And from his letters:

April 5, 1849: *To Evert Duyckinck*: "All ambitious authors should have ghosts capable of revisiting the world, to snuff up the steam of adulation, which begins to rise straightway as the Sexton throws his last shovelfull on him.—Down goes his body and up flies his name."

April 23, 1849: *To Lemuel Shaw*: "These attacks are matters of course, and are essential to the building up of any permanent reputation—if such should ever prove to be mine. . ."

June 1, 1851: *To Hawthorne*: "What 'reputation' H.M. has is horrible. Think of it! To go down to posterity is bad enough, any way; but to go down as a 'man who lived among the cannibals'! When I speak of posterity, in reference to myself, I only mean the babies who will probably be born in the moment immediately ensuing upon my giving up the ghost. I shall go down to some of them, in all likelihood."

Dec. 10, 1862: *To Samuel Savage*: "I once, like other spoonies, cherished a loose sort of notion that I did not care to live very long. But I will frankly own that I have now no serious, no insuperable objections to a respectable longevity. I don't like the idea of being left out night after night in a cold church-yard."

The concept of the post-self is, of course, directly related to the notion of annihilation. To cease as though one had never been, to be "oblivionated," to accept defeat, to abandon any hope of love or fame, any hope of impact or memory-in-the-mind-of-another beyond one's death, to be obliterated, to be ostracized, to be muted, to be naughted, to be expunged from history's record—that is a fate literally far worse than death.

Not unexpectedly, Melville had a few things to say on these issues:

Lightning-Rod Man: "Think of being a heap of charred offal, like a haltered horse burned in his stall; and all in one flash!"

Israel Potter: "Few things remain . . . He was repulsed in efforts after a pension by certain caprices of law. His scars proved his only medals. He dictated a little book, the records of his fortunes. But long ago it faded out of print—himself out of being—his name out of memory."

Redburn: "But all is now lost; I know not who he was; and this estimable author must need share the oblivious fate of all literary incognitos."

White-Jacket: "it is a good joke, for instance, and one often perpetrated on board ship, to stand talking to a man in a dark night-watch, and all the while be cutting the buttons from his coat. But once off, those buttons never grow on again. There is no spontaneous vegetation in buttons."

Pierre: "Unendurable grief of a man, when Death itself gives the stab, and then snatches all availments to solacement away. For in the grave is no help, no prayer thither may go, no forgiveness thence come; so that the penitent whose sad victim lies in the ground, for that useless penitent his doom is eternal, and though it be Christmas-day with all Christendom, with him it is Hell-day and an eaten liver forever."

From his letter to Hawthorne, June 1, 1851: "Though I wrote the Gospels in this Century, I should die in the gutter."

Implicit in the preceding is a board hypothesis, the contents of which run roughly as follows: that aspects of Melville's personality are to be found distributed (in either a direct or a refractory way) among his fictional characters; and further, there is implied a refinement of this general notion in the specific sub-hypothesis which proposes that within particular books there can be found a range of characters some of whom reflect a particular segment or portion of Melville's personality, and who, in their totality may yield the entire secret combination that unlocks the tantalizing safe. Related to this latter hypothesis is an article by the Italian critic Eugenio Montale (*Sewanee Review*, LXVIII, Summer 1960, 419-422) which mentioned, but certainly does not endorse—nor do I—the interpretation that the three principal characters of *Billy Budd* stand as different "narcissistic projections of the three ages of the author." More to the point and better documented: Professor Bezanson, in his "Introduction" and discussion of "The Characters" in the Hendricks House edition of *Clarel*, plausibly and convincingly advances the proposition that several of the main characters were intended to represent different aspects or potentialities of Melville's nature, and—what is especially relevant to our own present concerns—specifically that Mortmain embodied Melville's wish for self-annihilation. I quote, liberally, from Professor Bezanson: ". . . in the two decades after *Moby Dick*, Melville's descent into self had made him acquainted with an underworld of recalcitrant shades: the sense of defeat, willful isolation, unmanageable moods, fear of death, anxiety over his own physical and mental health . . . These darker elements of Melville's sensibility are channeled into the striking series of monomaniacs who followed one another so ominously through the poem: . . . From his first appearance Mortmain is committed by name ('Death Hand') and symbol (his black skull cap) to *self-annihilation.* The roots of his personal malaise, running subtle and deep, have flowered into political, philosophic, and religious despair . . . Consumed by psychic fury, driven to *intolerable introversion*, Mortmain has no strength left to hold back his own will to self-destruction."

I assume that every student of Melville is well acquainted with Professor Murray's explication of Melville's psychological positions over time in relation to his own annihilation. Quoting from Dr. Murray, they go something like this[7]:

In *Mardi* (1847), Melville's position was: "If I fail to reach my golden haven, may my annihilation be complete; all or nothing."

In *Moby Dick* (1851); "I forsee my annihilation, but against this verdict I shall hurl my everlasting protest."

In *Pierre* (1852): "I am confronted by annihilation, but I cannot make up my mind to it."

In 1856, in London, as recorded by Hawthorne: "I have pretty much made up my mind to be annihilated."

And in *Billy Budd* (1891): "I accept my annihilation."

After Melville's early successes with *Typee* and *Omoo*, and the excitement of his being challenged for veracity and for his criticism of missionaries, but not for his style nor genre nor philosophic exploration, when he dared then to write his first real romance and turned, after the first one hundred pages of *Mardi*, to the infinite perspectives of his own ruminations and discovered, as consequence, that he was met with a grape-shot barrage of annihilating criticism, the issue for him was forever joined.

Thereafter, his most vital dialogue of the mind concerned itself with whether or not he could fully live, express himself openly, be printed publicly, be read widely, be adjudged fairly; or whether he would need to print himself privately, eschew critical support, retreat from public view, write to his own soul's need—all partial deaths of his talents, his energies, his natural desires, and his interplay with his own time.

Out of Melville's combination of his great sense of inner pride, his bravura inner life style, his imperious reaction to hostility and to criticism, his conscious and unconscious attrition of the social side of his literary life—out of all of these diverse elements grew his concern with death and annihilation and his enormous investment in his post-self. In this sense, Melville wrote not so much for his own time as he did for any appropriate (that is, any appreciating) time to follow—for what Leyda has called a "posthumous celestial glory." Melville was partially dead during much of his own life, but he more than compensated for that lugubrious limitation by writing in such a way that he could realistically plan to live mostly after he had died. "On life and death this old man walked."

HOWARD P. VINCENT

12. "And Still They Fall from the Masthead"

FELLOW MELTHORNIANS—or should it be Fellow Haw-villains?

Trying to read a manuscript at the Kennedy Inaugural, Robert Frost faced the antagonisms of cold, light glare, bad handwriting, and old age, but that was all; he had on his side 70,000,000 viewers who liked him and who may have known one of his poems but nothing about poetry. Anyone who dares address this congress this weekend has friendlier physical conditions than did Frost—but oh! the psychological ones, for he must face a fine-feathered flock of specialists who know 191 times more than he does. I feel especially sympathetic to the "newer" group facing this flock, the group which I define as doves, the older ones having long ago revealed themselves as hawks.

The hawks are here, impressively, in covens and in gams. You doves must flutter before that perch of predatory birds. I classify the hawks hastily in three groups: first, the editors, the vultures—Bezanson, Bruccoli, Ferguson, Foster, Gilman, Hayford, Mansfield, Roper, Sealts, and Wright; then there are the kestrel critics—all the just-cited plus Bowen, Cowie, Fogle, Hillway, Howard, Miller, plus others ad infinitum—all of you; and then there are two rare birds in this present aviary, two awesome eagles capable of thunderbolt descents: the Peckham which in its rage for chaos soars beyond tragedy; and that Catskill eagle who dives into abysses and then circles towards the sun, Henry Murray, a bird to make any Jung dove easily Freudened.

I may have my own fears, but I admit, white hair to the contrary, that I am no dove. I am perhaps to be termed, as is now obvious, a windheaver. All I can do is to say: "I have swum through Melville and sailed through Hawthorne; I have had to do with Pittsfield and with Lennox with these visible hands; I am in earnest, and I will try. There are some preliminaries to settle."

II

"And Still They Fall from the Masthead." The title is my recollection of a line from Virginia Woolf (the real one, not the Albee one), and its charm rests upon the word "still." In general, the title refers to Melville's deep and lifelong affection for masthead sitting and sitters, honored especially in a notable chapter of *Moby-Dick*—an affection shared, in his cool way, by Melville's friend Hawthorne. The title next refers to *White-Jacket* in general, most particularly to Chapter 92 where White-Jacket's dramatic fall into the speechless profound of the sea is the climax of Melville's genial and tough book. Finally, the title ("still") means that the book and especially the Fall passage stays with me even after years of scholarly and critical exorcism; I am again falling from a masthead from which I thought, more than a year ago, I had taken my last tumble.

Perhaps, to be simple, the title means that I am determined to talk about *White-Jacket* because few other people have done so, at least not at length nor in detail. *White-Jacket* may not be Melville's unread book, but I estimate it to be one of the least studied, the least critically examined, of the Melville canon. There are but a few short treatments of the book (and most of the writers of those studies are here today), and only one is a critical essay. There is no book (although one just-finished doctoral dissertation). If I sound a bit aggressive, bear with me. The chip on my shoulder may fall off at the end of this hour.

Since this is a friendly conference, a few personal words may not offend. Mine has been a long encounter with Melville's fifth book. It began more than 25 years ago and its first result was a paper entitled, "*White Jacket.* An Essay in Interpretation." I suggested then that *White-Jacket* should be read with an open mind, that it should be read as something more than the documentary which it so eminently is, and as something more than mere realism, which also it most emphatically is. I argued the half-palpable presence in the book of an unrecognized dimension, metaphysical and symbolic, centered largely in the creation, the career, and the fate of the ridiculous white jacket with which the book opens, to which on several comical occasions it returns, and with which it ends in the Fall from the Yardarm. I then suggested what I have in my book since demonstrated in great detail, that the man who found himself so fully in *Moby-Dick* was enabled by the writing of *White-Jacket* to develop and establish his powers as a writer and as a perceiver (for the two roles may not be separated) in order to write *White-Jacket*, and that *White-Jacket* contained in imminence the mastery of *Moby-Dick*.

I will admit that my finding in that little essay scarcely ranked with Ahab's sighting of the white whale, nor, say, with Murray's sighting of Melville here in this hall fifteen years ago, in "In Nomine Diaboli," but at least my essay directed the attention of the world—maybe ten readers at the most—to an element in *White-Jacket* which those ten lonely enthusiasts may have previously missed. More important for me was that the essay was but a beginning of a love affair with *White-Jacket*, for it soon led to my fatal seduction, for in time I went the whole way and gave my all—to a full scale book, arrived at by experiences which I may not relate here. In *The Tailoring of Melville's White-Jacket*, now snailing through the press, I bore down on *White-Jacket* as though it were the world's supreme masterpiece, tracking sources with obsessive zeal, and noticing every trick of Melville's practiced and practicing pen, until I seemed a man demented, that book my whale and I an Ahab. Above all, I filled almost 100 pages in an examination of the three pages of Chapter 92 in which the narrator, White-Jacket, plummets from the yardarm into the speechless profound of the sea, thence to rise and to be rescued by his mates. Since the scene was the narrative climax of a book otherwise comparatively unnarrative, and completely plotless, and since, well, since it was a great piece of prose, I made and make no apology for my hundred pages piled upon its back. You might say that I gave that passage the full treatment—the works.

Many of you are well aware of your inability to find your way out of Melville's labyrinthine world. This can be good, this can be bad. Some scholars have gone mad while wandering the mazes. *Circumspice*. I wish to insist, however, that during my 25 years of fun and games in the library stacks with Herman, I have, in this matter of

White-Jacket, always kept my cool. Never have I said that *White-Jacket* is a great book. There are fond parents who can discriminate as well as dote—who know that their little Rollo is no genius even if he is a dear.

No, *White-Jacket* is not a great book; it is not a major book, but it is a good book and it has great things in it. It was, however, a major book in the creative growth of Herman Melville, not simply because it preceded *Moby-Dick* but because by writing it Melville made discoveries about himself and his art which significantly served him for the future. Most of us naively think that books are written primarily to amuse or to inform us. They aren't, that is the great books aren't that primarily. They are part of the progress of the poet himself. Camus put it well: "But perhaps the great work of art has less importance in itself than the ordeal it demands of a man and the opportunity it provides him of overcoming his own phantoms and approaching a little closer to his naked reality." Melville could write *Moby-Dick* because he had written *White-Jacket*. To place the books side by side and to study their resemblances, which are many, and their differences, which are even greater, is to behold potential against fulfillment, restraint against release, timidity against daring—all in the most striking of diptychal relationships.

Melville himself, you will recall, was slightly scornful of both *White-Jacket* and *Redburn*, but this was the self-annoyance and irk that you might feel had you spent precious hours darning your husband's old socks when you might better have been finishing that stunning evening dress for the Annual Cotillion. What bugged Melville was that *White-Jacket* was not what he most deeply wanted to do, or at least, to do in exactly that way. "And all my books are botches." Here is one of my "ifs" of literature: If Herman Melville had let himself go—that is, had he been fully released as he was a year later by reading *Mosses from an Old Manse*—and had he then tried to extract poetry from ship's planks as later he extracted it from blubber, had he developed a narrative line, a plot—that is, had he novelized the strong, explosive materials of the *Neversink* life, he would have produced his first masterpiece in the summer of 1849 and not the spring of 1851.

What is *White-Jacket* about? A glib and specious explanation might be made—and generally is—that the subject of the book is life on board a man-of-war. That, certainly, is the alternate title given on the title-page, and it is, so far as it goes, appropriate. Nine-tenths of the book *is* devoted to the details of life on the "Old Wagon," the *Neversink*; no battleship in the United States Navy has ever been more vividly documented. White-Jacket-Melville takes us on a touristic stroll around the frigate to show us its physical structure, its human hierarchies, its ultimate and evil purpose, but he does this not simply to inform but also to indict. He considers the consequence of this ship society in terms of human suffering and sacrifice, of hypocrisy and brutality in general and of psychological disintegration in particular. It is not just about a man-of-war world, but it is a metaphor for our general man-of-war-ish world. This, Melville implies, is my world—and welcome to it. The Church (Chaplain and worship), the Law (Articles of War), and Society in its hivelike complexity are exposed and condemned by Melville's relentless camera work. Read attentively, *White-Jacket* is quite a book; it has both bulk and bite.

This granted, nevertheless *White-Jacket* is not "about" life on or in a man-of-war. Melville himself never said so, although his preface carefully admitted that his own "man-of-war experiences" had been incorporated in his pages. The book was titled by Melville, and we should respect his titling.

That is another matter. Melville called his book *White-Jacket.* Had the subject been life in a man-of-war he might have called it "From Orlop Deck to Yardarm," or maybe "Naval Life as Seen by a Novice." He didn't; he called it *White-Jacket.* The title quite clearly refers both to the narrator and to his grotesque jacket. The man-of-war world is very much there—indeed, the world is too much with us—but what the book is about is how White-Jacket sees his world and what he does with it, what it does with him. *White-Jacket* is title and subject.

But now to the jacket. Melville wrote in comic desperation, "Jacket, jacket, you have much to answer for," and taking the statement seriously I have found several "answers" for it. Somewhere in his champagne-heaven Melville may be muttering, "Vincent, Vincent, you have much to answer for."

Traditionally the jacket has been explained (on those rare occasions when some Martian has deigned to consider it) as a kind of comic continuity lightly imposed on an otherwise discontinuous documentary.

It has also been regarded as an amusing diversion for the reader racked by the brutal realities, especially the floggings, which are so prominent in the book. These views are as valid as they are safe and sound, but they do not suffice. Readers who have been ready to look philosophically and free-wheelingly at Gogol's overcoat, at the asses' skin in Balzac's novel, at a red cloth letter A, or at the pair of shoes in *Waiting for Godot*, have averted their minds from the potentialities of Melville's "not very white" jacket. You might think that no one had ever read *Sartor Resartus*, or then, having read it, he had not seen how profoundly that book had instructed Melville.

In my essay of long ago my main explanation of the jacket was that it was a symbol similar in purpose and meaning to, say, the prosy old guide book which failed Redburn in Liverpool. The white jacket was constructed to protect White-Jacket from the elements, especially during the difficult days when they would round the Cape. It failed in every way and on two occasions it was almost the death of its wearer. In other words, you must not rely blindly on the guides of the past, the constructions from the past, the myths and fables handed you by father and mother, priest and lawyer—they may or may not be valid, but you must in the shaping of your ultimate self depend on that self—you.

In my book, however, I became more specific to show how much Melville used the construction of the jacket as a parody in metaphor of his own methods of writing (as well as of his own process of individuation). Melville was mocking the method by which all of his previous books had been built, and when his hero rips the jacket from him to let it sink into the sea, Melville is rejecting even old literary forms—for we must constantly recognize Melville's technical originality—and he is expressing a determination to find his own way through life and through literature—a blended, braided thing. Wallace Stevens' rejection of poeticisms in "Montrachet-le-Jardin" conveys the same point rather elegantly:

> Bastard chateaux and smoky demoiselles,
> No more. I can build towers of my own,
> There to behold, there to proclaim, the grace
>
> And requiting of responsive fact,

To project the naked man in a state of fact
As acutest virtue and ascetic trove.

III

But now to take two new tumbles from that yardarm.

Tumble One: the Fall from the Yardarm is Melville's first and most formidable statement of vocation; formidable even though veiled beneath the narrative disguise, or formidable because it is veiled, implied to us rather than being rudely and crudely phrased.

There were two important stages in Melville's development as an artist: first was in his deciding to become a writer, and second was in his deepened recognition of what being a writer, in the Shakespearean or Hawthornian sense, meant. The decision to become a writer was probably made during the last leg of Melville's sailor voyage home from the South Seas. There is no "evidence" of this except Melville's own statement, which I take seriously and almost literally. When he wrote to Hawthorne in words now famous, "From my twenty-fifth year I date my life. . ." and then proceeded to describe creative unfolding, growth, I must, in the absence of contrary evidence, take it that at some moment during the homeward voyage (or shortly after arrival home in October) Melville underwent an identity crisis and came to a radical decision about vocation which affected him—and the world—forever.

Where, incidentally, was (just to be finically literal) Melville on his twenty-fifth birthday, August 1, 1844? He was a sailor on board the frigate *United States* cruising comfortably through calm and prospering seas with good supporting breezes, in latitude 54.35 S and longitude 58° 07 W. Nothing important happened that day on board the ship, or at least nothing important was reported in the ship's log except the usual conditions of wave and weather. No ships were sighted, no men were flogged, and certainly no one fell overboard. Captain Sterling might well have said, "It is a mild day, Starbuck." For the sake of our fiction-fact, let us thus pinpoint, tongue slightly in cheek, this very day as the date for what truly took place somewhere along this time: Melville in confronting his return home determined no longer to be an omoo but to be an artist. We have his word that something happened, and I suggest that the Fall passage in *White-Jacket* recounts symbolically not only that moment of self-discovery but also, and just as important, his discovery of depth psychology, or better for us, depth literature. This statement is not mere pun. The Fall passage fulfills the statement from the letter, and describes veiledly the emergence of the writer from the talented scribbler. The Fall passage dates, probably, from late summer 1849, and was a pre-conscious statement of what Melville came to consciously in July 1850 when, reading *Mosses from an Old Manse,* he fell from the spectator role of journalist into the depths of the involving and monster-ridden sea.

The Fall, then, was Melville's coming to consciousness not of the external world, for that he had seen abundantly in his unusual travels, but of the interior world which he called "the world of mind," the chartless world for which the artist creates the charts. There comes a time when looking must modulate into understanding, and this was the moment for Melville.

There came a time in the history of western civilization—in the mid- and late-nineteenth century when the imagination had to confront and describe the interior world, the psyche. Admittedly, the discovery of the psyche as an object of systematic study is one of the great achievements of human history, and the nineteenth century may be credited with this dazzling and disturbing discovery. It is interesting to entertain the possibility that this Fall passage from *White-Jacket* is the first time in American letters that the unconscious and its special significance to man has been described. Except for a passage from Proust and a paragraph from Henry James which I have used elsewhere, the most remarkable professional description of what takes place in the Fall experience of *White-Jacket* is found in a paragraph by Carl Jung:

> When the libido leaves the upper world of light, whether by individual decision, or owing to the decline of vital energy, it sinks back into its own depths, into the source from which it once flowed out, and returns to the point of cleavage, the navel, through which it once entered our body. This point of cleavage it called the "mother," for it is from her that the source of the libido came to us. Therefore, when there is any great work to be done, from which the weak human being shrinks, doubting his

> own strength, his libido streams back to that source—and that is the dangerous moment, the moment of decision between destruction and new life. If the libido remains caught in the wonderland of the inner world, the human being becomes a mere shadow in the upper world: he is no better than a dead man or a seriously ill one. But if the libido succeeds in tearing itself free and struggling up to the upper world again, then a miracle occurs, for this descent to the underworld has been a rejuvenation for the libido, and from its apparent death a new fruitfulness has awakened.

Certainly, with Herman Melville after *White-Jacket*, and partly because of *White-Jacket*, a new fruitfulness was awakened. From this time Melville was a new and matured writer, no longer content with journalistic dexterities and with Defoesque documentaries. More than a mere cloth garment (Melville told Dana that it had been "a veritable garment") slid into the Atlantic Ocean (the "veritable garment" into the Charles River); it was a garment through which Melville was assisted to self-fulfilment.

More may be made of the Fall, but at the moment you may feel like Monsieur Jourdain, who in asking what the two pseudo-Turkish words "Ben men" meant, was given the fake translation, "He requests that you go with him at once to prepare for the ceremony, so that he may then meet your daughter and conclude the marriage." Amazed, Jourdain replies, "All that in two words!" and Corvielle explains, "Yes. That is what the Turkish language is like. You can say a great deal in a few words."

Such concentrations of meaning were not haphazard as a quick glance at the text will show. There is, for instance, a special artistry in the unusual way in which in the three pages of the Fall from the Yardarm he gathers together in one scene the central images of his, subsequently, greatest art, images which in the previous four books and through most of *White-Jacket* had been popping up here and there asking to put into some significant pattern or relationship one to another. That relationship, for instance, which they find in *Moby-Dick*. Now they find that relationship. They are (1) the ship, (2) the unplumbed, salt, estranging sea, (3) harpoons and whale line, (4) coiled monsters and fashionless forms, (5) falling and breaching, height and depth, and (6) finally, by metaphoric extension, the naked authentic self, the essential psyche. It is a remarkable stock-taking, and not accidental although maybe intuitive. In the Fall from the Yardarm Melville gathered about him the important gear of his profession like a Bulkington readying himself for a whaling voyage to unknown lands. As he was.

IV

Tumble Two.

A second, significant conclusion to be drawn from Melville's Fall from the Yardarm follows when and if one accepts the argument that Melville has persistently used the clothing metaphor to refer to composition. In the Fall, however, the Carlylean fooling terminates and a new seriousness appears, as the jacket vanishes into the ocean the serious artist breaches into the sunlight. The Fall is, however, the climax to a process which has been operating throughout the book, now to achieve a new seriousness, a new intensity. In *White-Jacket* we have Melville's personal entrance into his poem, the poet in the poem. This is the second strong sign of modernity in a book which might seem otherwise old-fashioned, tradition-shaped.

The problem of the poet in the poem is a modern one, at least made modern by the new emphasis given it by the developing insights and discoveries of psychology and anthropology, and a problem anticipated, accepted, and then exploited by poets of all media. In general, writers before 1798 (each of you has his own date, depending which work you determine as the *point de depart*—all right, if you demand 1781 take it), writers before 1798, writers of the well-bred sort (Laurence Sterne wonderfully not so) held to Aristotle's view that "The poet should say very little *in propria persona.*" No "modern work" respects that dictum, or, doing so, stays classified as a modern work. Modern poets are everywhere in their poems, and their poems are ever about poetry; it is the mark of their modernity. What I am trying to say has been said perfectly by our finest poet in three short stanzas from "An Ordinary Evening in New Haven":

This endlessly elaborating poem
Displays the theory of poetry,

As the life of poetry. A more severe,
More harassing master would extemporize
Subtler, more urgent proof that the theory
Of poetry is the theory of life,

As it is, in the intricate evasions of as,
In things seen and unseen, created from nothingness,
The heavens, the hells, the worlds, the longed-for lands.

A delightful issue of this Conference during these three days has been how, happily, it has become related to some kind of heavenly time, to chronometrical sightings. Nevertheless, the harsh, ticking, minute-bound world of horologicals imperiously commands terminations, not permitting me the development of some thoughts relating to the subject of the poet in the poem which Melville himself delightfully recognized and contained, consciously, in the third chapter of *Moby-Dick*, when, describing the painting over the bar at the Spouter Inn, Melville described the very book he was writing, acknowledged its difficulties of meaning and interpretation, and anticipated the future actions and bewilderments of readers and critics of the novel.

Fortunately, your familiarity with this passage allows me to curtail discussion of it; for now I will describe it as a document evidencing Melville's consciousness of his poetic art and of its operative place in his writing. Melville here says in effect, addressing posterity: "Gentlemen, whatever you say about my whaling book may be true, but you must also recognize that I too know what it is about, or at least I know what I was doing, even though I may not have entirely succeeded according to my Platonic ideal. I wish in this painting metaphor to assert that the book it adorns is the act of a consciousness, alert if not Jamesian, and it is not the haphazard reminiscences or unthinking fumblings of a pen pushed by tar-stained fingers. I, Melville the maker, am in and throughout my poem, and I have made poetry the subject (or one of the major subjects) of the work. I have shown this awareness and this strategy in the guises of a sub-sub librarian and a pale usher; I have made a literary classification of whales; I have employed constructional talk in many places, openly posing to you my immediate problems. In doing this I have shaped myself, in the constant process of becoming which works of art demand from the poet.

Will there be not stopping place? Lord, when when shall we be done changing? I could, as a spirit haunting your conference, quote a French poet I read the other day in one of your journals—in fact, I will:

L'écrivain
Dans sa cage
J'écris
Ces mots
Qui m'écrivent."

Thus spoke the spirit of Melville. I must conclude my talk, sadly omitting treatment of our other tutelary spirit, Nathaniel Hawthorne, simply mentioning in passing his similar, insightful recognition of creative process as the subject of his poetry, an awareness which I perceive in the use he made of the little scarlet letter which he describes, utilizes, in the Custom House Sketch prefaced to *The Scarlet Letter*. Maybe some other day, "Something further may follow of this Masquerade."

Meantime, concluding in a rush, I leave in a wonderment and amazement that from mid-summer 1849 to mid-summer 1850, give or take a few months, three pieces of cloth were utilized (created) which have assumed significant places in the fabric of American letters. One, the first, was a roughly stitched, much patched jacket full of useless pockets; the second was a canvas daubed with cross-hatchings of paint almost like an abstraction; and the third was a crimson letter three and one-quarter inches high. These objects return to our memory with happy frequency; they are jars in Tennessee which help to bring our psychic wildernesses into some kind of order. They are works of artifice contained in great works of art and they celebrate the redemptive power of the creative imagination, of art itself. America of 1850 much needed such celebrations, such reminders, and she was fortunate in getting three such delightful ones.

Notes to the Text

CHAPTER 7 / J. Donald Crowley

[1] Seymour L. Gross and Randall Stewart, "The Hawthorne Revival," in *Hawthorne Centenary Essays*, ed. Roy Harvey Pearce (Columbus, Ohio, 1964), p. 343.

[2] Randall Stewart (ed.), *The American Notebooks of Nathaniel Hawthorne* (New Haven, 1932), p. xix.

[3] *Ibid.*, p. xlii.

[4] *Ibid.*, p. xv.

[5] *Ibid.*, p. xiii.

[6] Randall Stewart, "Editing *The American Notebooks*," *Essex Institute Historical Collections* (July, 1958), p. 278.

[7] "A Note on Hawthorne's Revisions," *Modern Language Notes*, LI (November, 1936), p. 426. Professor Turner implies here that Hawthorne's marriage to Sophia preceded the publication of the 1842 *Twice-Told Tales*. The fact is, however, that the second edition was published in January, 1842, and the marriage did not take place until July 9, half a year later. Since Hawthorne had to see to the revisions and proofreading in late 1841, it is less than likely that Sophia played a part in the changes made for the collection.

[8] "Hawthorne's 'Vision of the Fountain' as a Parody," *American Literature*, XXVII (March, 1955), pp. 101-105.

[9] See *The Blithedale Romance* (Centenary Edition, 1964), pp. li-liii.

[10] *Ibid.* Bowers notes that although "the deletions undoubtedly represent [Hawthorne's] final intentions, the causes behind these intentions are suspect."

[11] *Loc. cit.*

[12] *Ibid.*, p. 279.

[13] This manuscript is in the New York Public Library.

[14] *The Token* (1832), p. 225.

[15] Stewart, *The American Notebooks*, p. xv.

[16] *New-England Magazine* (December, 1834), pp. 401-402.

[17] Cited in Terence Martin, *The Instructed Vision* (Bloomington, 1961), p. 37.

[18] Randall Stewart, *Nathaniel Hawthorne* (New Haven, 1948), p. 56.

[19] Stewart, *The American Notebooks*, p. xv.

[20] Hawthorne to W. D. Ticknor, June 7, 1854. Cited in *Letters of Hawthorne to W. D. Ticknor, 1851-1864* (Newark: Carteret Book Club, 1910), p. 8.

[21] The extent to which Hawthorne was indeed anonymous is dramatically illus-

trated by the fact that the Pittsfield (Massachusetts) *Sun*, reprinting "The Shaker Bridal" (November 16, 1837), could attribute the story to "MISS SEDGWICK."

22 F. O. Matthiessen, *American Renaissance* (London and New York, 1941), p. 203.

CHAPTER 8 / John H. McElroy

1 William Charvat *et al.*, eds. *The Scarlet Letter, Centenary Edition of the Works of Nathaniel Hawthorne*, I, (1962), p. 4. In all cases page citations after the first appear in the text.

2 My study of Puritan novels, from the inception of this sub-genre of American historical novels to the Civil War, indicates that this stereotyped conception of the Puritan was clearly formulated and fostered by American novelists three generations before the advent of H. L. Mencken. Some of those novelists surpassed even Mencken's vehement disapproval of the repressive aspect of Puritanic society, but usually, as in Hawthorne's novel, an attempt was made in the early nineteenth century to counter the stereotype of the repressive Puritan with instances of "human" behavior. (*Images of the Seventeenth-Century Puritan in American Novels, 1823-1860*. Unpublished dissertation, Duke University, 1966.)

3 William Leete Stone, *Mercy Disborough* (Bath, N.Y., 1837), p. 50.

4 anon., *The Salem Belle* (Boston, 1842), p. 214.

5 anon., *The Witch of New England* (Phila., 1824), p. 214.

6 Eliza Buckminster Lee, *Delusion* (Boston, 1840), p. 114.

A CHRONOLOGY OF PURITAN NOVELS
PUBLISHED IN AMERICA BEFORE *THE SCARLET LETTER*

1823 James McHenry, *The Spectre of the Forest*
1824 Harriet Vaughan Cheney, *A Peep at the Pilgrims*
Lydia Maria Child, *Hobomok*
anon., *The Witch of New England*
1825 anon., *The Christian Indian*
1827 Catherine Maria Sedgwick, *Hope Leslie*
1828 John Neal, *Rachel Dyer*
1829 James Fenimore Cooper, *The Wept of Wish-ton-Wish*
1831 Delia S. Bacon, *The Regicides*
1834 William Leete Stone, *Mercy Disborough*
1839 Rufus Dawes, *Nix's Mate*
1840 Eliza Buckminster Lee, *Delusion*
1842 anon., *The Salem Belle*
1845 Henry William Herbert, *Ruth Whalley*
1848 Eliza Buckminster Lee, *Naomi*
1849 John Lothrop Motley, *Merry Mount*
James Kirke Paulding, *The Puritan and His Daughter*
John Greenleaf Whittier, *Margaret Smith's Journal*
1850 Nathanial Hawthorne, *The Scarlet Letter*

CHAPTER 9 / Albert McLean

[1] W. H. Auden, *The Enchafed Flood* (New York, 1950).

[2] Herman Melville, *Moby Dick, or, The Whale*, eds. Luther S. Mansfield and Howard P. Vincent (New York, 1952), p. 105.

[3] Merlin Bowen, *The Long Encounter* (Chicago, 1960), p. 125.

[4] Melville, *op. cit.*, p. 9.

[5] *Ibid.*, pp. 37-38.

[6] *Ibid.*, p. 29.

[7] *Ibid.*, pp. 10-11.

[8] *Ibid.*, pp. 38-39.

[9] *Ibid.*, p. 74.

[10] *Ibid.*, pp. 161-62.

[11] *Ibid.*, pp. 46-48.

[12] *Ibid.*, p. 105.

CHAPTER 10 / F. De Wolfe Miller

[1] I am grateful to Clifford E. Barbour, Jr., of Knoxville, Tennessee, and Nantucket, for calling my attention to the unique copy of the first issue of the Nantucket *Daily Telegraph* which he purchased at a local auction, and for his considerable help in gathering other material for this essay.

[2] Only one copy of each edition is known to the Library of Congress Union Catalog: the copyright deposit at the Library of Congress and the second edition at Harvard.

[3] Charles Feidelson, Jr., ed., *Moby-Dick*, (Indianapolis, 1964), p. 729.

[4] Merton M. Sealts, Jr., *Melville's Reading* (Cambridge, Mass., 1950), p. 276.

[5] In the American Experience Series, New York, 1963. Edouard Stackpole has included reproductions of the astonishing woodcuts from Comstock's version. It is from his introduction that we learn that Lay returned on the *United States*.

[6] Not, of course, to be confused with Capt. Coffin.

[7] Eleanor Melville Metcalf, in her edition of Melville's *Journal of a Visit to London . . .* (Cambridge, Mass., 1948), p. 170.

[8] Janez Stanonik, *Moby Dick: The Myth and the Symbol* (Lubljana, 1962), pp. 32-41.

CHAPTER 11 / Edwin S. Shneidman

[1] Litman, Robert E., Curphey, Theodore J., Shneidman, Edwin S., Farberow, Norman L., and Norman D. Tabachnick. "Investigations of Equivocal Suicides," *Journal of the American Medical Association*, 1963, Vol. 184, 924-929.

[2] Shneidman, Edwin S., "Orientations toward Death: A Vital Aspect of the Study of Lives," in Robert W. White (Ed.), *The Study of Lives*. New York:Atherton Press, 1963; reprinted with discussion in the *International Journal of Psychiatry*, March, 1966, Vol. 2, 167-200.

[3] Murray, Henry A., "Dead to the World: Or the Passions of Herman Melville in Edwin S. Shneidman (Ed.), *Essays in Self-Destruction,* (to be published).

[4] Shneidman, Edwin S., "Suicide, Sleep and Death: Some Possible Interrelations among Cessation, Interruption and Continuation Phenomena." *Journal of Consulting Psychology,* 1964, Vol. 28, 95-106.

[5] My great appreciation to Miss Jan Kramer of the Los Angeles Suicide Prevention Center for her enormous effort and help in this connection, is here expressed.

[6] "Sleep and Self-Destruction: A Phenomenological Approach," in *Essays in Self-Destruction* (to be published).

[7] Henry A. Murray, "Introduction," *Pierre, Or The Ambiguities,* New York: Henricks House (Farrar Straus), 1949, pp. xiii-ciii.

Appendix

THE PROGRAM OF THE MELVILLE-HAWTHORNE CONFERENCE

Friday, September 2nd

3:00-6:30 p.m. Special Exhibit, the Chapin Library of Williams College

Arranged by H. Richard Archer

Refreshments 5:00-6:30 p.m.

7:00 p.m. Opening Dinner, Greylock Dining Hall

Presiding: Luther S. Mansfield, Williams College

Welcome: John W. Chandler, Dean of the Faculty, Williams College

Response: Henry A. Murray, Harvard University, President of the Melville Society

8:30 p.m. Evening Session, Adams Memorial Theatre

Presiding: Henry A. Murray

"Early Days in the Melville Society," Tyrus Hillway, Colorado State College at Greeley

"Hawthorne and a Third Culture," Harold C. Martin, Union College

10:00 p.m. Social Hour, Faculty House

Saturday, September 3rd

9:00 a.m. Morning Session, Adams Memorial Theatre

Presiding: Walter E. Bezanson, Rutgers University

"The Structure of Encounter: Melville's Review of Hawthorne's *Mosses,*" John D. Seelye, University of Connecticut

"Melville: Berkshire Visions," Henry A. Murray

10:30 a.m. Buses leave for tour of Monument Mountain, Stockbridge, Hawthorne's "Red House," picnic at Tanglewood

2:30 p.m. Berkshire Athenaeum: Special Exhibit

Arranged by Robert G. Newman

Melville Memorial Room: Honoring Eleanor Melville Metcalf and Henry K. Metcalf

Henry A. Murray and Paul C. Metcalf

Visit to Melville's "Arrowhead," through the courtesy of Mrs. Hale Holden

4:30 p.m. Hancock Shaker Community

Presiding: Mrs. Lawrence K. Miller

Sketches and songs from Leonard Kastle's new opera, *The Pariahs*

Thomas E. O'Connell, Berkshire Community College, Mrs. O'Connell, and Mrs. Miller

Chorus directed by Andrew W. Clarke

6:00 p.m. Cocktails and Dinner, Hancock Shaker Community

9:00 p.m. Social Hour, Faculty House

Sunday, September 4th

9:00 a.m. Morning Session, Adams Memorial Theatre

Presiding: William H. Gilman, University of Rochester

Richard H. Fogle, University of North Carolina

"The Conventionality of *The Scarlet Letter*," John H. McElroy, University of Wisconsin

"Hawthorne in his Letters," Norman Holmes Pearson, Yale University

"The Artist as Mediator: The Rationale of Hawthorne's Revisions," J. Donald Crowley, University of Delaware

"Hawthorne and Melville as European Writers," Morse Peckham, University of Pennsylvania

12:00 noon Buses Leave for Pittsfield

1:00 p.m. Luncheon at Melville's "Broadhall," now the Pittsfield Country Club

Presiding: Luther S. Mansfield

2:30 p.m. By way of Lake Onota, Balance Rock, and Lake Pontoosuc, return to Williamstown in time for those who wish to pay a short visit to the Sterling and Francine Clark Art Institute

5:30 p.m. Cocktails, Faculty House

7:00 p.m. Dinner, Greylock Dining Hall

8:30 p.m. Philip Hanson in his solo performance of *Moby-Dick* Adams Memorial Theatre

10:00 p.m. Social Hour, Faculty House

Monday, September 5th

9:00 a.m. Morning Session, Adams Memorial Theatre

Presiding: Merton M. Sealts, Jr., University of Wisconsin

Elizabeth Foster, Oberlin College

"Another Chapter in the Story of the Great White Whale," F. DeWolfe Miller, University of Tennessee

"Spouter Inn and Whaleman's Chapel: Cultural Matrices of *Moby-Dick*," Albert F. McLean, Jr., Transylvania College

"And Still They Fall from the Yard-Arm," Howard P. Vincent, Kent State University

"The Deaths of Herman Melville," Edwin S. Shneidman, Chief, N.I.M.H. Center for Studies of Suicide Prevention

12:45-1:15 p.m. Luncheon, Greylock Dining Hall Cafeteria

1:45 p.m. Afternoon Session, Adams Memorial Theatre

Presiding: Nathalia Wright, University of Tennessee

" 'Character', 'Nature', and Allegory in *The Scarlet Letter*," Seymour Katz, University of Massachusetts at Boston

"The Scarlet A, Gules, and the Black Bubble," Maurita Willett, University of Illinois at Chicago

Epilogue: Luther S. Mansfield

Conference Committee for the Melville Society

Mrs. Hale Holden

Mrs. Lawrence K. Miller

Lawrence K. Miller
Henry A. Murray
Robert G. Newman
Thomas E. O'Connell
Howard P. Vincent
Wyllis E. Wright
Luther S. Mansfield, *Chairman*

Index